Better Homes and Gardens®

DOLLAR · STRETCHING DECORATING

BETTER HOMES AND GARDENS® BOOKS
Editor: Gerald M. Knox
Art Director: Ernest Shelton
Managing Editor: David A. Kirchner

Furnishings and Design Editor: Shirley Van Zante
Senior Furnishings Editor, Books: Pamela Wilson Cullison

Associate Art Director (Managing): Randall Yontz
Associate Art Directors (Creative): Linda Ford,
   Neoma Alt West
Copy and Production Editors: Marsha Jahns,
   Nancy Nowiszewski, Mary Helen Schiltz,
   David A. Walsh
Assistant Art Directors: Harijs Priekulis, Tom Wegner
Graphic Designers: Mike Burns, Alisann Dixon, Mike Eagleton,
   Linda Haupert, Deb Miner, Lyne Neymeyer, Stan Sams,
   D. Greg Thompson, Darla Whipple, Paul Zimmerman

Editor in Chief: Neil Kuehnl
Group Editorial Services Director: Duane L. Gregg

General Manager: Fred Stines
Director of Publishing: Robert B. Nelson
Director of Retail Marketing: Jamie Martin
Director of Direct Marketing: Arthur Heydendael

DOLLAR-STRETCHING DECORATING
Editor: Pamela Wilson Cullison
Copy and Production Editor: Nancy Nowiszewski
Graphic Designers: Lyne Neymeyer, Bill Shaw

Introduction

Almost everything costs a lot these days, and home furnishings are no exception. But steep prices needn't stand in the way of decorating and furnishing your home to your utmost satisfaction.

In the realm of interior design, imagination counts more than the size of one's bank account. And, as Better Homes and Gardens® *Dollar-Stretching Decorating* will show you, there are hundreds of ways to sidestep high costs without having to scrimp on style or settle for less in terms of quality, comfort, or function.

Whether you're just starting out in your first house or apartment, or simply in the mood to improve or update a tired-looking room, you're sure to be inspired by the wide assortment of ideas and do-it-yourself projects included in this book.

Contents

chapter

1
Buying Right

There's no denying that it takes money to decorate a home. Just how much it takes is the question. Does the size of one's bank account determine the success of a decorating scheme? Must one sacrifice beauty, comfort, or quality in order to keep the lid on home furnishings costs? The answer to both questions, happily, is "no." It is quite possible to create an eye-pleasing environment without going to any great expense or having to be constantly on the lookout for bargains.

Actually, there's no big secret involved in furnishing a room, or even an entire home, on a budget. What *is* involved, mostly, is common sense and a willingness to become a shrewd shopper.

One of the wisest things you can do is to acquaint yourself with the basic elements of good design. Try to expose yourself to as many design influences as possible: museums, art galleries, fine furniture stores, books, and magazines. In other words, train your eyes. You may not

be able to afford the very best, but at least you'll be able to recognize well-designed furniture, fabrics, lamps, and accessories when you see them. Good proportions, pleasing lines, and quality workmanship are not, after all, the exclusive domain of high-priced, top-of-the-line furnishings. Indeed, just because something is expensive doesn't mean that it's necessarily worth owning. Conversely, just because something is inexpensive doesn't mean that it's second-rate. The real measure of an object's worth—be it a chair, a table, or a lamp—lies in how useful or pleasing it is to the person who owns it, and how well it fits, literally and figuratively, in the home.

Good design is meaningless unless the furniture you choose complements the room in which you plan to use it, and, more importantly, unless it makes sense for the way you actually live. Function and comfort should always come first. What good, after all, is a picture-perfect room if it doesn't make you (and your family and guests) feel at home? The first and foremost purpose of good design, then, is to enrich our lives—not just the appearance of our surroundings.

Decorating on a budget does not mean that you must do without, or settle for second best. Depending on how strapped you are for funds, you may have to put off certain purchases until a later date, but there's nothing wrong with that. Few people can afford to furnish and decorate a room all at once, nor should they try to. By far, the most pleasing rooms are those that develop over a period of time. So if you're just starting out with your first house or apartment, remember that patience pays off in the long run.

Bargain hunting can also pay off, but only if you know how to avoid the pitfalls. Evaluate sales carefully. A sale item is not a bargain unless you will really use and enjoy it. Refrain from buying on impulse, and never buy anything simply because the price is greatly reduced.

Whatever you do, avoid the temptation to buy a roomful of furniture at rock-bottom prices. Tune out those television commercials that promise three rooms of furniture for practically nothing. As the old saying goes, "You get what you pay for." There's no point in spending a penny on furnishings that are doomed to soon fall apart.

You'll be better off (and so will your bankbook) if you make it a point to always buy the best you can afford. This may entail buying a single, good-quality piece (such as a sofa) and making do with inexpensive "interim" pieces (such as canvas deck chairs) until you're able to afford the other furnishings you want. Many kinds of casual and outdoor furniture can serve well indoors as attractive interim pieces, then later be moved to the patio or porch. Also, don't overlook today's well-designed plastic furnishings and accent pieces that you assemble yourself. The styling and quality of both have greatly improved in recent years. The same is true for unfinished furniture items that you paint or stain to suit your decor.

Because the furnishings business is a seasonal one, you can save as much as 50 percent if you buy off-season. Furniture sales usually take place after Christmas and again in July and August when business is slow and stores are preparing for manufacturers' new lines.

You'll also do well to explore specialty shops, import stores, discount warehouses, and mail order outlets for good-quality furnishings at reasonable prices.

And, of course, there are often terrific bargains to be found at auctions, flea markets, secondhand shops, and garage sales. Here again, take care not to buy something just because the price is right.

Another good way to save money when decorating, whether you're starting from scratch or redoing an existing room, is to break away from preconceived notions and "rules." There is no law, for instance, that says a dining room must be furnished to the hilt with traditional dining room pieces—full-size table, matching chairs, china cabinet, and buffet. The fact is, most rooms, especially in today's smaller homes, would look and function much better with less furniture squeezed into their already-cramped spaces.

Still another notion that needs dispelling is the one that says a room isn't "right" unless all the furnishings pieces match or are of the same period or style. Actually, rooms furnished *en suite* tend to look contrived and boring, and they can be costly as well. Try to steer clear of a matched look that limits your buying options. Instead, devise a decorating plan that allows you plenty of latitude in terms of what you buy and how much you spend.

Keeping your options open also gives you more leeway in developing your own personal decorating style. The most interesting and inviting rooms are those that reflect their owners' personalities and tastes. Surround yourself with your favorite things. If you're a collector, let it be known. Unleash your imagination and open your thinking to new possibilities. It's through imagination that old lace tablecloths become delightful new curtains, quilts and homemade craft items become colorful works of "art," and a bowl of fresh fruit or vegetables becomes a charming (and edible) centerpiece for the dining table.

Planning Ahead

chapter

2

Room arranging is one of the few decorating endeavors that costs nothing at all. Without spending a single cent, you can instantly make any room more functional, comfortable, and inviting—simply by rearranging the furniture you already have. So, don't jump to the conclusion that your room needs redecorating. It may well be that it's only the arrangement—not the furniture—that needs replacing.

Before you begin shuffling your furnishings (even on paper), give some thought to how you want your rooms to function. Are there ways you'd like to improve the use of space? Think carefully. Perhaps there are activities you'd like to include that your rooms can't accommodate right now. For example, have you always wanted a writing desk or reading chair in your bedroom but haven't been able to find the space? Do you have a bulky desk or piano that's creating an obstacle course? Or do you need to centralize your assortment of stereo gear?

In addition to simply finding the square footage for your favorite activities, you may want to subdivide the space so that each function you include has its own well-defined, even if small, area.

Rooms that have a natural focal point are by far the easiest to arrange for optimal function and flexibility. By creating a conversation grouping around the focal point—a fireplace, a handsome window wall, or an interesting architectural element—you're free to use the remaining space for other purposes. If, for example, you have a family room with a wall system as a focal point, you may want to create a seating group around the wall unit. You can isolate the conversation area by turning the backs of two chairs or a sofa to the rest of the room. Behind this seating group, you may find room for a table that serves nicely for desk work or casual meals. You may even find that you have space left over for an exercise bicycle or an artist's easel.

If your room has no natural focal point, you can easily create one. Try adding a large poster or a wall-hung afghan or quilt, floor-to-ceiling bookshelves, or one large furniture piece, such as an armoire.

ENLARGE BY EDITING

In your effort to make better use of space by rearranging existing furnishings, remember the alternative: elimination. Just because you've always included this or that chair, table, or other furniture item in a particular room doesn't mean you're locked into keeping it there. As you plan the arrangement, evaluate your possessions. For instance, do you have a chair that no one ever sits on or a curio cabinet that collects nothing but dust? If so, you may find that you can create a more expansive room arrangement by selling the item or moving it to another room.

TRY SOMETHING NEW

There's more to furniture arranging than eking out extra space. The way you arrange your furnishings can actually help minimize a room's awkward proportions, make a small space seem larger, or cozy up a too-large room.

To visually make the most of space, take a good look at your room's assets and liabilities, then make an effort to play up the good points and minimize the bad ones.

While making a reassessment of your present furniture arrangement, give some thought to out-of-the-ordinary configurations, such as diagonal groupings. Furniture arranged on a diagonal can visually widen a narrow space and break up the boxiness of a plain, square room. Diagonal groupings also can "tilt" the floor plan to take advantage of a special feature, such as a fireplace or a beautiful view. In a long, narrow room, de-emphasize the elongated proportions by creating an "island" seating arrangement in the center of the room.

The floor plans in many homes are such that they force people to walk right through the center of the living room to get elsewhere in the house. Short of remodel-

ing, there are several ways to improve the situation. One solution is to place a sofa perpendicular to the wall, thus creating the semblance of a corridor. Still another way to redirect traffic is to buy or build a freestanding shelf unit, and place it wherever you need a new "wall."

SEPARATE AREAS

If your problem is a too-large room, consider breaking it into two or three separate areas. In a large living room, for example, capitalize on the space by creating two or more intimate conversation groupings, or make room for a private study or reading corner. Area rugs do an excellent job of defining space in a large room. And, assuming the colors are compatible, you can place area rugs directly on top of carpet.

In a spacious bedroom, use a screen, a freestanding shelf unit, or a ceiling-hung curtain panel to separate a dressing room or a home office from the sleeping area.

USE VERTICAL SPACE

When it comes to furniture arranging, small rooms in general—and small bedrooms in particular—are especially irksome. After all, a 9x10-foot room is still a 9x10-foot room, no matter how clever the arrangement. There are things you can do, however, to make a small room less claustrophobic. Your best bet, in addition to limiting the amount and size of furniture, is to take advantage of vertical space. In a small bedroom, use even a sliver of vertical space for stacking storage units. Or nestle your bed between built-in shelves. Instead of using a long, low dresser, use a tall one such as a highboy. Take advantage of alcoves, too. A small niche can be fitted with shelves, and a dormer can be turned into a compact office with a wall-mounted, flip-down desk.

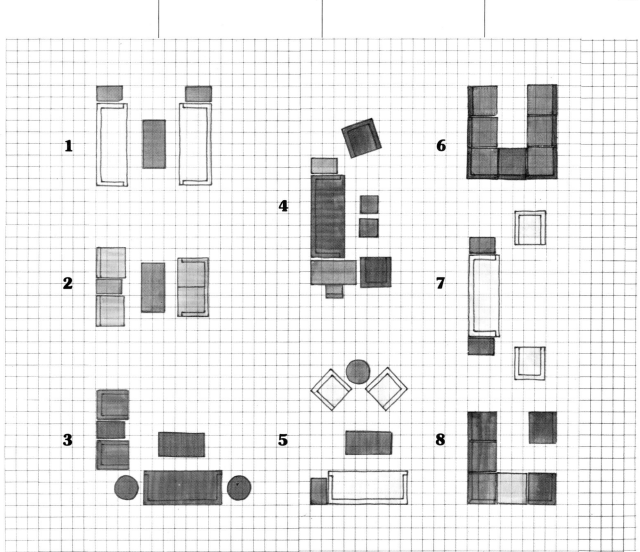

GOOD CONVERSATIONS

Are you short on ideas for arranging your living room or family room furniture? Here are eight conversation groupings to consider. Note how most of them utilize similar major seating pieces.

1. A large room can benefit from the "weight" of a grouping like this one. Twin standard-size sofas sit opposite each other, with lamp tables placed at one end only and a cocktail table in the center. In a smaller room, twin love seats could be used in a similar fashion. A face-to-face arrangement looks very handsome in front of a fireplace.

2. If your living room is too small for a full-size sofa, try a modest-size grouping like this one. Two modular seating units face a love seat, with a cocktail table conveniently located in between.

3. An L-shape seating arrangement is especially useful for directing traffic *around* a conversation grouping instead of right through it. This right-angle arrangement includes a standard three-cushion sofa and two lounge chairs separated by a narrow table.

4. Here's another L-shape grouping with a slightly different twist. Instead of using two matching end tables at the ends of the sofa, substitute a desk for one of the tables. The desk serves double-duty as an end table and a space-saving work surface. Two small bunching tables in front of a sofa replace a single, large table. Two chairs complete the grouping.

5. This classic arrangement looks attractive in front of a picture or bay window. A pair of matching lounge chairs, positioned at an angle and served by a small round table, faces the sofa and a rectangular coffee table.

6. Modular seating pieces offer exceptional versatility and flexibility in living rooms, family rooms, and open-plan schemes. Buy as few or as many modulars as you want to fit your space and seating needs. In this illustration, five modular pieces—one corner unit and four armless chairs—are arranged in an informal grouping.

7. A symmetrical furniture arrangement is well suited for a narrow living room or any room where space is in short supply. Here, two matching lounge chairs are placed at right angles to the sofa, forming a compact and intimate conversation grouping. The narrow end tables that serve the sofa also serve the chairs, eliminating the need for a coffee table.

8. Either in a fairly small room or in a large open-plan space, try grouping modular or sectional seating pieces around a low table, as shown.

PLANNING ON PAPER

Too often, we think of furniture arranging and rearranging as frustrating exercises designed to try our spirits—and strain our backs. But it doesn't have to be that way. By preplanning on paper, you can experimentally position and reposition your furnishings without lifting a finger. Included here and on the following four pages are graph paper and furniture templates to help you arrange your rooms for the utmost in comfort, function, and convenience.

Planning on paper can do a lot more than save your back; it can save money, too. By giving thought to such things as room size, furniture dimensions, traffic patterns, placement of radiators, windows, doors, and other seemingly mundane matters, you're far less likely to make costly mistakes when purchasing new items for your home. In addition, by planning ahead, you're far more likely to make the best use of every square inch of space.

HOW TO DRAW A FLOOR PLAN

To begin your plan, use the graph paper provided, *opposite,* as your scale guide. (One square or ¼ inch equals one foot.) Lay a sheet of tracing paper over the graph paper. Measure your room carefully, and sketch its outline on the tracing paper, showing the walls to be 6 inches thick. Be sure to indicate windows and doors (and the directions in which they swing), all electrical outlets, telephones and telephone jacks, light switches, cable television entry point, and even furnace vents

and cold-air returns in the floor and walls. Also indicate any architectural features, such as a fireplace, an arched opening, a built-in buffet or bookshelves, and sliding or folding doors. Use a fresh sheet of tracing paper for each room in the house.

NOTE TRAFFIC LANES

After you've drawn your room plans, stop and think about the "paths" you and your family seem to naturally take—into, out of, and through the room. Must you walk through the room to get to another one? Is there a deck, patio, or solarium doorway that must be taken into account? You'll want to allow about 2 feet (two squares of graph paper) for each traffic lane. As you plan your furniture groups, try to arrange them so they won't be disturbed by—or impede—traffic passing through the room.

The same guidelines apply to door openings. Be sure to leave at least a 3-foot clearance at all doorways and try to allow 4 feet at an entrance.

USING THE TEMPLATES

Beginning on page 16, you'll find templates of a wide variety of furniture items for most every room in the house. Find the templates that come closest to the size and shape of your own furniture, then trace and cut them out. (Width and depth are indicated on each piece.) Unless you have an extremely tight space problem, don't worry if a cutout differs by 2 or 3 inches from the dimensions of your furniture. If a piece of furniture fits none of the templates provided here, simply draw and cut your own, remembering that ¼ inch equals one foot.

Although it isn't absolutely necessary, you might find it helpful to have samples of your carpet, wall coverings, paints, and upholstery patterns for color reference.

STRIVE FOR BALANCE

You'll probably find it easiest to begin by placing your largest pieces on the plan. As a rule, when you need to use space efficiently, it's best to keep big items parallel or at right angles to the wall. As you arrange the furniture, keep balance in mind so that heavy pieces are not all in one part of the room and light ones in another.

In addition to balance, keep scale in mind—that is, the size relationship of one piece to another. While you can add interest to any room by varying the scale of items, don't overpower a small item by placing a large one beside it. Pattern and color should be balanced, too. By coloring templates with crayons or pencils, you'll be able to tell at a glance where to repeat certain colors and patterns.

Table height is an important consideration in both dining and living areas. The average dining table is 29 inches high and usually requires a chair with an 18-inch seat height. On the other hand, a game/party table is 25 inches high and requires a lower chair height and additional leg room around it. While end tables usually are 19 to 22 inches high and coffee tables vary from 15 to 18 inches high, those numbers can—and should—vary, depending on the height of your sofas and chairs.

Also, keep proportion in mind when choosing lamps. A small end table will be dwarfed by a too-massive lamp, while a generous-size table may need a large lamp for balance. Let your eye be your guide.

ALLOW SPACE FOR PEOPLE

Don't forget to allow space for people to get into and out of seating groupings. Try to plan for at least 15 inches of leg room between a sofa or chair and a coffee table and at least 3 feet of space around the perimeter of a dining table. Keep in mind the guideline to allow at least 2 feet for traffic lanes.

Of course, you don't want to space furniture too far apart, either. Place tables within easy reach of sofas or chairs, and try to arrange the seating pieces so that people can converse easily. (Studies have shown that people feel most comfortable in face-to-face versus side-by-side conversations. However, sociability tends to decrease if the distance between two people is more than 5 feet.)

ADD FLEXIBILITY IN SMALL ROOMS

If space is at a premium in your home, your best bet is to plan your rooms for multi-purpose living. Careful planning and arranging can help you get maximum use of the space you have. Here are some ideas:
• Define living areas by placing a large piece of furniture at a right angle to the wall to form a divider.
• Push a large dining table against the wall when its full size is not needed, or use a drop-leaf table.
• Remember to choose furnishings with flexible uses. Nests of tables, stacking storage units, modular seating pieces, and tables that incorporate storage space in them are versatile furnishings items. Look for multipurpose wall systems that incorporate drop-lid desk space or built-in drop-down tables.
• To save precious floor space, hang bookshelves or other kinds of storage units. Create budget-priced bedside tables that take up no floor space by bolting store-bought or homemade cubes to the wall on either side of the bed.

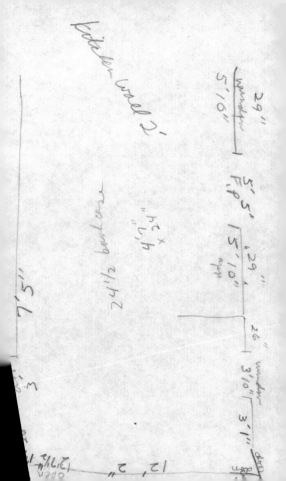

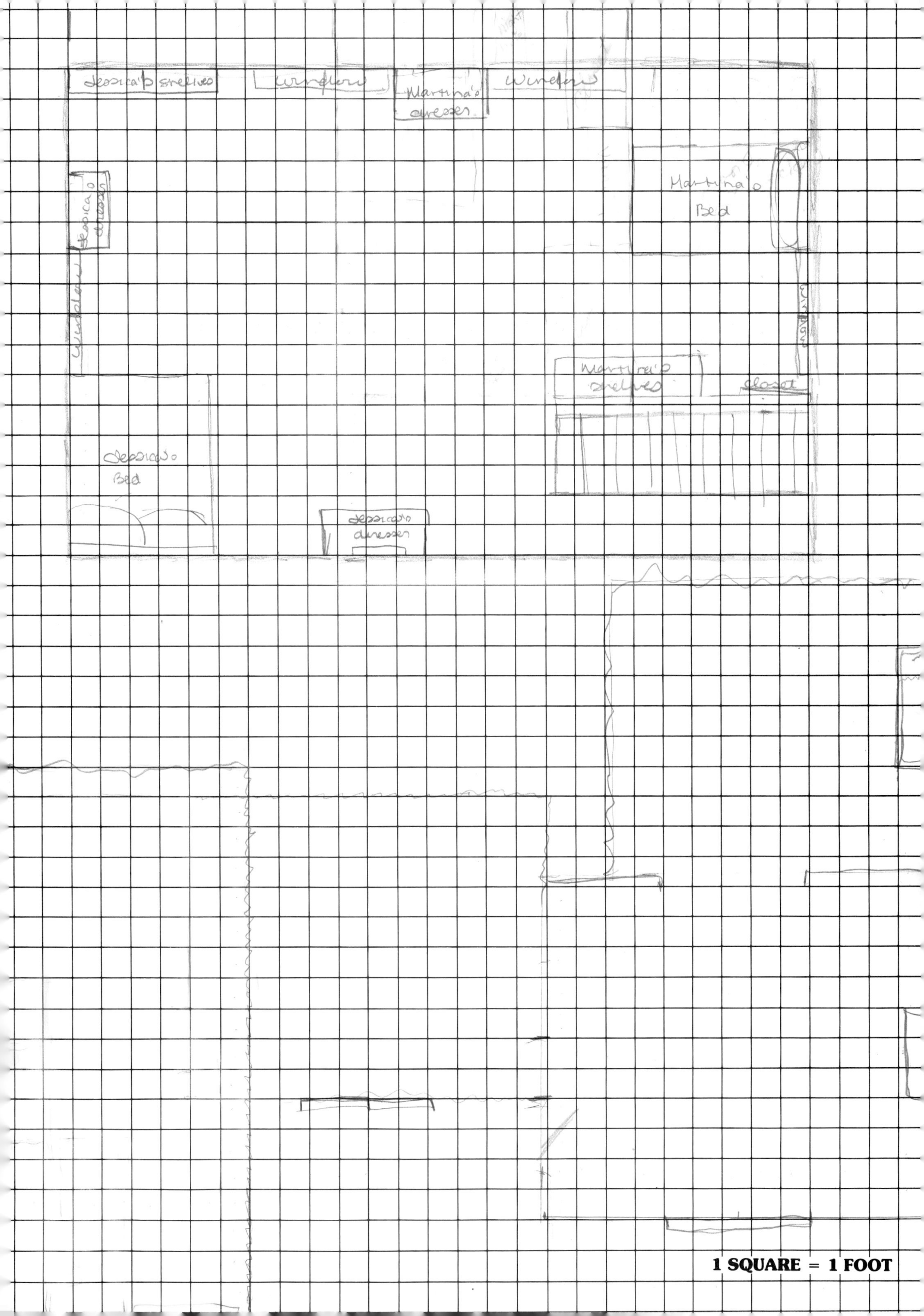

Jessica's shelves   Window   Martina's dresser   Window

Jessica's dresser

Window

Martina's Bed

Window

Jessica's Bed

Martina's shelves   closet

Jessica's dresser

1 SQUARE = 1 FOOT

FURNITURE TEMPLATES

UPHOLSTERED FURNITURE

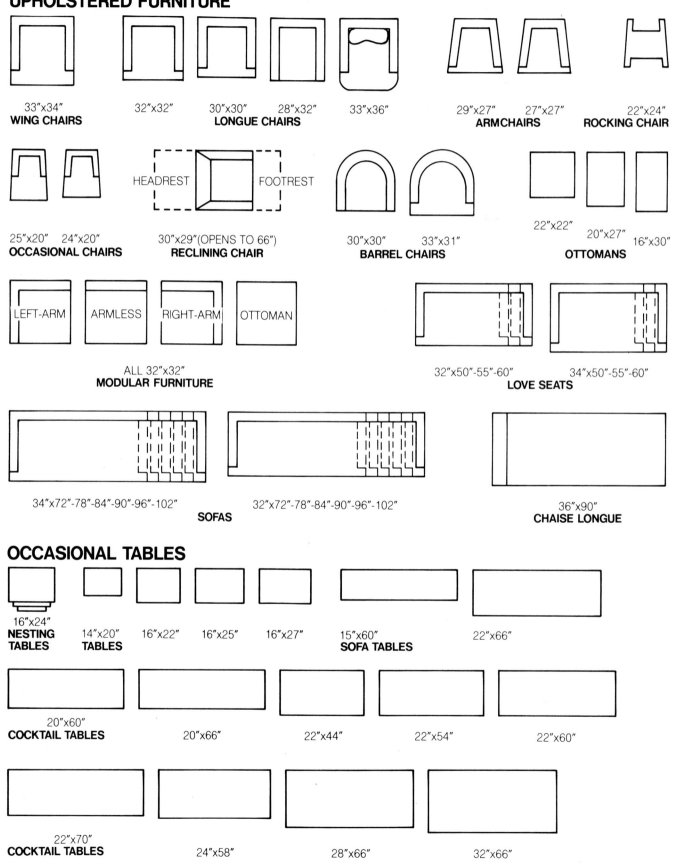

33"x34"
WING CHAIRS

32"x32"   30"x30"   28"x32"
LONGUE CHAIRS

33"x36"

29"x27"   27"x27"
ARMCHAIRS

22"x24"
ROCKING CHAIR

25"x20"   24"x20"
OCCASIONAL CHAIRS

HEADREST   FOOTREST

30"x29"(OPENS TO 66")
RECLINING CHAIR

30"x30"   33"x31"
BARREL CHAIRS

22"x22"
20"x27"   16"x30"
OTTOMANS

LEFT-ARM   ARMLESS   RIGHT-ARM   OTTOMAN

ALL 32"x32"
MODULAR FURNITURE

32"x50"-55"-60"
34"x50"-55"-60"
LOVE SEATS

34"x72"-78"-84"-90"-96"-102"
SOFAS

32"x72"-78"-84"-90"-96"-102"

36"x90"
CHAISE LONGUE

OCCASIONAL TABLES

16"x24"
NESTING TABLES

14"x20"
TABLES   16"x22"   16"x25"   16"x27"

15"x60"
SOFA TABLES   22"x66"

20"x60"
COCKTAIL TABLES   20"x66"   22"x44"   22"x54"   22"x60"

22"x70"
COCKTAIL TABLES   24"x58"   28"x66"   32"x66"

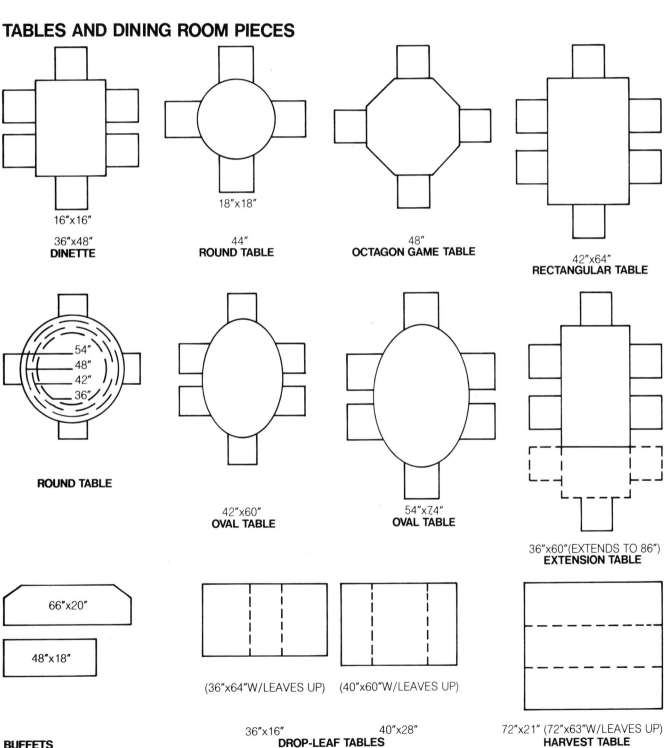

36″
28″
24″
20″
18″

SQUARE TABLES

40″
36″
24″
18″
12″

ROUND TABLES

TABLES AND DINING ROOM PIECES

16″x16″
36″x48″
DINETTE

18″x18″
44″
ROUND TABLE

48″
OCTAGON GAME TABLE

42″x64″
RECTANGULAR TABLE

54″
48″
42″
36″

ROUND TABLE

42″x60″
OVAL TABLE

54″x7.4″
OVAL TABLE

36″x60″(EXTENDS TO 86″)
EXTENSION TABLE

66″x20″

48″x18″

BUFFETS

(36″x64″W/LEAVES UP)   (40″x60″W/LEAVES UP)

36″x16″
40″x28″
DROP-LEAF TABLES

72″x21″ (72″x63″W/LEAVES UP)
HARVEST TABLE

SOFA BEDS, BEDS AND BEDDING

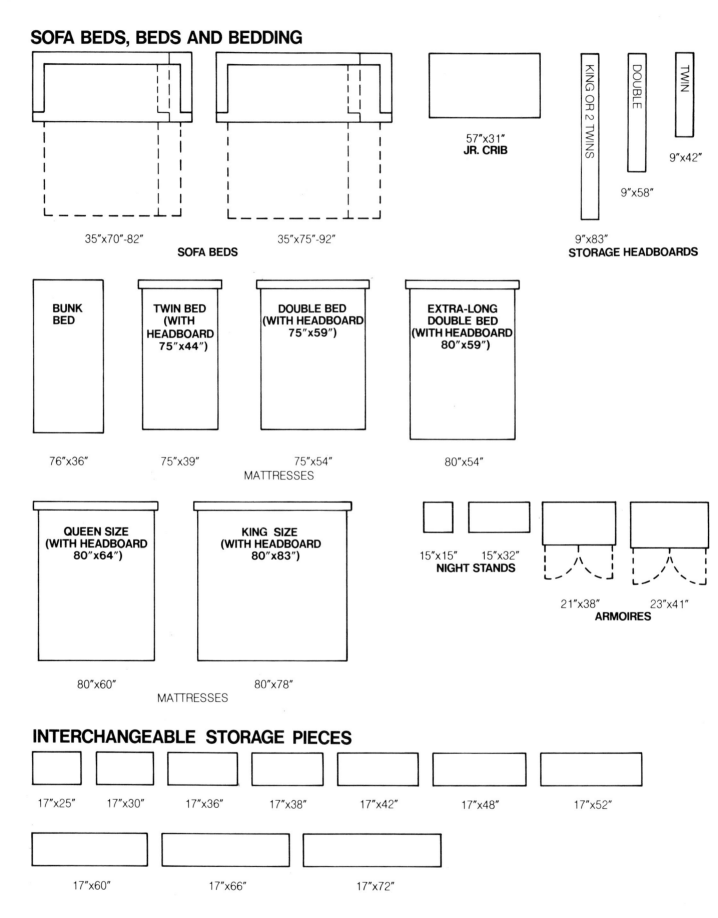

35"x70"-82"   35"x75"-92"

SOFA BEDS

57"x31"
JR. CRIB

KING OR 2 TWINS   DOUBLE   TWIN

9"x42"

9"x58"

9"x83"
STORAGE HEADBOARDS

BUNK BED

TWIN BED (WITH HEADBOARD 75"x44")

DOUBLE BED (WITH HEADBOARD 75"x59")

EXTRA-LONG DOUBLE BED (WITH HEADBOARD 80"x59")

76"x36"   75"x39"   75"x54"   80"x54"

MATTRESSES

QUEEN SIZE (WITH HEADBOARD 80"x64")

KING SIZE (WITH HEADBOARD 80"x83")

15"x15"   15"x32"
NIGHT STANDS

21"x38"   23"x41"
ARMOIRES

80"x60"   80"x78"

MATTRESSES

INTERCHANGEABLE STORAGE PIECES

17"x25"   17"x30"   17"x36"   17"x38"   17"x42"   17"x48"   17"x52"

17"x60"   17"x66"   17"x72"

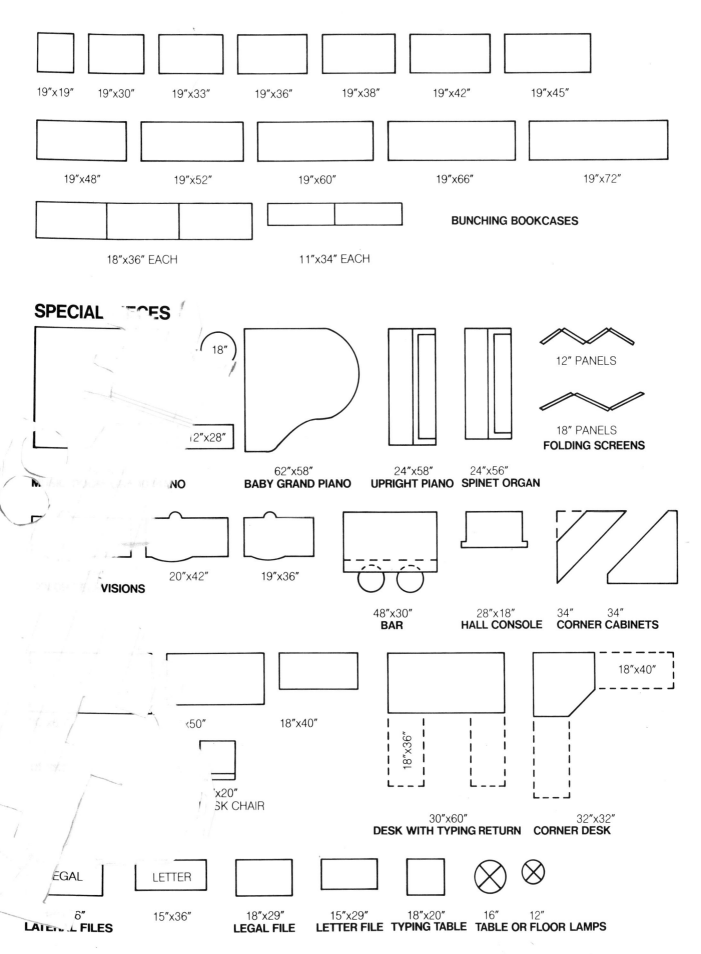

19"x19"   19"x30"   19"x33"   19"x36"   19"x38"   19"x42"   19"x45"

19"x48"   19"x52"   19"x60"   19"x66"   19"x72"

BUNCHING BOOKCASES

18"x36" EACH   11"x34" EACH

SPECIAL ᴵᶜᴱS

18"

12"x28"

12" PANELS

18" PANELS
FOLDING SCREENS

62"x58"   24"x58"   24"x56"
NO   **BABY GRAND PIANO**   **UPRIGHT PIANO**   **SPINET ORGAN**

20"x42"   19"x36"

VISIONS

48"x30"   28"x18"   34"   34"
BAR   **HALL CONSOLE**   **CORNER CABINETS**

18"x40"

50"   18"x40"   18"x36"

x20"
SK CHAIR

30"x60"   32"x32"
DESK WITH TYPING RETURN   **CORNER DESK**

EGAL   LETTER

6"   15"x36"   18"x29"   15"x29"   18"x20"   16"   12"
LATERAL FILES   **LEGAL FILE**   **LETTER FILE**   **TYPING TABLE**   **TABLE OR FLOOR LAMPS**

chapter

3
Style on a Shoestring

With the wealth of well-designed, moderately priced fabrics and furnishings available at retail today, there's no reason to let a shortage of funds sabotage your decorating plans. An option—if you're handy with a hammer and nails—is to utilize the do-it-yourself projects included in this book. By taking this approach, you'll not only save money, but you'll create a custom look as well.

Elegance on a budget" aptly describes the living room pictured here. Working with the natural assets of a high ceiling, statuesque windows, and a handsome, traditional fireplace, the owners created an uptown look on a strictly shoestring budget. With the exception of the two antique wooden tables, all of the furnishings and accessories in the room are new and moderately priced.

A major decorative statement is made by using two chaise longues in lieu of conventional sofas. The chaises are constructed of solid foam, and—in addition to providing sophisticated seating—they fold out into standard-size beds. The sleek-lined chair

does double-duty, too. Designed to be used outdoors as well as in, the chair is stylishly at home in this setting.

Other money-saving ideas in this well-appointed room include the sisal floor covering and the simple matchstick blinds at the windows. The vertical paper lantern to the right of the fireplace serves not only as a source of light but as a contemporary sculpture as well.

Theoretically, you could furnish a room like this one in just a couple of hours. Most of the furnishings, including the chrome and glass coffee table, are stock items that can be carried home from the store the same day you find them.

Ingenuity is the answer when your decorating dreams are bigger than your bankbook. By using a little imagination, you can find good, workable solutions for any number of decorating problems.

Take your pick of the inventive ideas in the apartment pictured *above,* for instance.

Consider first the sofa. Looking for all the world like the high-priced variety, it's actually a single bed in disguise. Simple directions on how to make it are provided on the opposite page. If you happen to live in a studio apartment, a daybed/sofa provides a smart solution for saving both money and space.

Canvas deck chairs—the kind you'd expect to see at the beach or around a pool —are excellent alternatives to upholstered chairs. These sling-seat beauties have their own headrests and can't be beat for comfort. Deck chairs can be yours for a fraction of the cost of conventional seating pieces without sacrificing on style. Canvas director's chairs offer a similar seating solution.

For the price of plywood and a can of black paint, you can make a slick cube coffee table like this one. Check the how-to directions, *opposite.*

There's no reason at all to deprive yourself of attractive

artwork—no matter how pinched you are for funds. Here a 4x6-foot terry-cloth beach towel—stapled to a canvas stretcher frame and hung on the wall—adds color to the scene for minimal cost. On the adjacent wall, a large, unframed poster provides additional eye appeal.

Bath towels turn up again as plushy covers for pillows on the daybed.

Window treatments can be a major expense in any decorating scheme. One way to cut costs is to take any large piece of fabric (such as the Indian cotton bedspread shown here), staple the fabric to a wood strip nailed to the

top of the window frame, then slip a dowel through the bottom hem for weight. This type of fabric treatment offers privacy at all times without totally blocking the light.

CUBE COFFEE TABLE

Making the contemporary black cube coffee table is easy. Begin by building a cube *(diagram at right)* using ¾-inch plywood or particleboard. Once the cube is complete, paint the piece with semigloss enamel in the color of your choice, or cover with plastic laminate. These days, working with plastic laminate is easy. Two tools—a tile and laminate cutter and a laminate edge trimmer—are all you need. First, using a straightedge, score through the finished surface of the laminate with the cutter (cut the pieces slightly oversize so you can trim them later). Next, lay a block of wood along the line and snap the laminate toward you to break. After cutting, brush a coat of nonflammable contact cement onto one surface of the wood base and the back of the corresponding laminate piece. Let both pieces dry. Then, using dowels to keep the two surfaces apart, start at one edge, stick it down, and work toward the far edge, pulling out dowels as you go. Repeat this procedure for all sides.

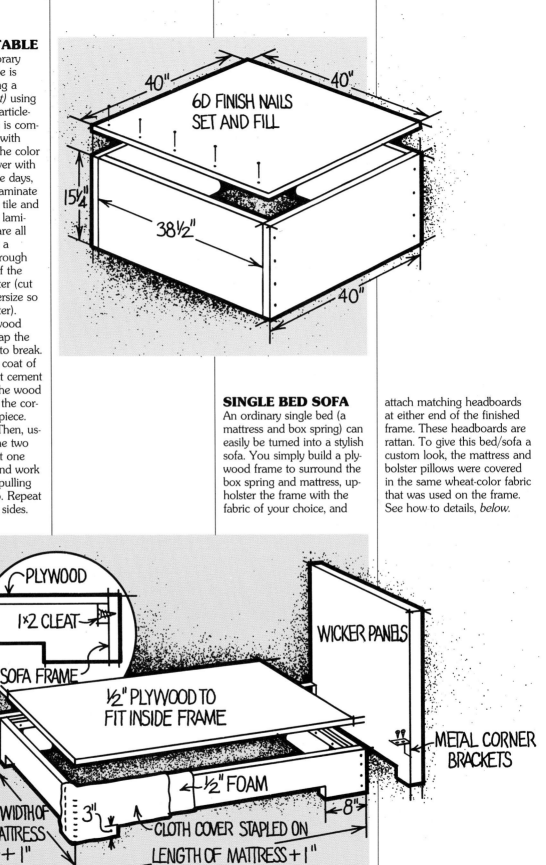

40" 40"

6D FINISH NAILS SET AND FILL

15¼" 38½"

40"

SINGLE BED SOFA

An ordinary single bed (a mattress and box spring) can easily be turned into a stylish sofa. You simply build a plywood frame to surround the box spring and mattress, upholster the frame with the fabric of your choice, and attach matching headboards at either end of the finished frame. These headboards are rattan. To give this bed/sofa a custom look, the mattress and bolster pillows were covered in the same wheat-color fabric that was used on the frame. See how-to details, *below*.

PLYWOOD

1×2 CLEAT

SOFA FRAME

WICKER PANELS

½" PLYWOOD TO FIT INSIDE FRAME

METAL CORNER BRACKETS

½" FOAM

WIDTH OF MATTRESS + 1"

3"

CLOTH COVER STAPLED ON

8"

LENGTH OF MATTRESS + 1"

Located in a turn-of-the-century firehouse, this living room once was home to a fire engine. By combining imagination with elbow grease, the owners transformed the former fire station into a charming dwelling. Renovating an old structure can save a considerable amount of money on housing costs, especially if you do much of the work yourself.

Against the old-fashioned background, the contemporary furnishings are a real standout. Only the tongue-and-groove paneling is truly original—everything else in the room is newly purchased or is homemade.

The stacked seating system was designed to save space as well as money. Simple to make, it consists of three twin-size mattresses, professionally upholstered in blue cotton fabric, stacked on sisal-covered plywood platforms. Two plywood boxes, also covered with the sisal matting, serve as end tables for the sprawl-inviting arrangement, while lots of plump pillows covered in a variety of interesting fabric remnants add to the comfort.

A bleached pine coffee table and two picnic-basket chairs complete the compact grouping. Underscoring the stylish scheme is a new wide-plank pine floor and a straw beach mat used as a rug.

You can attain decorating success on many levels by building this platform seating system. What makes this handsome system different from most others is that it's modular—and therefore, mobile—a boon for apartment dwellers and anyone who moves often.

Depending on the size of your room and whether you want to create an island effect or a multi-level "landscape," you can build the platforms either 6 or 12 inches high. Each island defines a functional area and gives you a lift to see the view. Build (or buy) as few or as many flexible modulars as you need.

Shown here is a wooden "bridge" that serves no other purpose than to visually connect two of the island areas. It consists of a frame made with 2x4s and a series of 1x2s spaced ¼ inch apart. The frame and the spacers are connected to a sheet of ¾-inch plywood for support. Exposed bolts and washers hold the unit together.

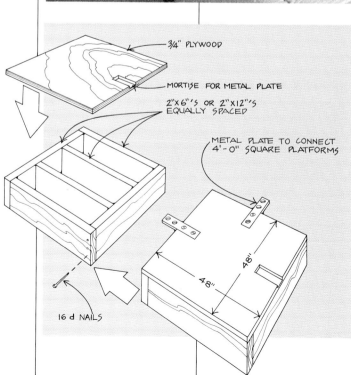

¾" PLYWOOD

MORTISE FOR METAL PLATE

2"X6"'S OR 2"X12"'S EQUALLY SPACED

METAL PLATE TO CONNECT 4'-0" SQUARE PLATFORMS

48"

48"

16 d NAILS

PLATFORM UNITS

Although it's not possible to provide a platform plan tailored to your room, the drawing *at left* shows the general construction method that can be adapted to any situation. The secret is to keep platform modules no longer than 4 feet by 4 feet. Make 4x4 squares to fill up most of the space, then tailor smaller pieces to fit where needed. Join all the modules with metal plates as shown, recessed into the surface of the plywood. When the modules are connected, staple on carpet, or if you prefer, have it professionally installed.

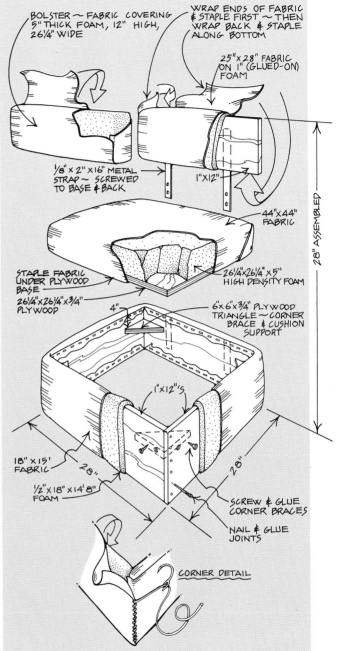

BOLSTER ~ FABRIC COVERING 5" THICK FOAM, 12" HIGH, 26¼" WIDE

WRAP ENDS OF FABRIC & STAPLE FIRST ~ THEN WRAP BACK & STAPLE ALONG BOTTOM

25"x28" FABRIC ON 1" (GLUED-ON) FOAM

⅛" x 2" x16" METAL STRAP ~ SCREWED TO BASE & BACK

1"X12"

44"X44" FABRIC

28" ASSEMBLED

STAPLE FABRIC UNDER PLYWOOD BASE

26¼"x26¼"x¾" PLYWOOD

26¼"x26¼"x5" HIGH DENSITY FOAM

4"

6"x 6"x¾" PLYWOOD TRIANGLE ~ CORNER BRACE & CUSHION SUPPORT

1"X12"'S

18"X15' FABRIC

28"

28"

½"X18"X14'8" FOAM

SCREW & GLUE CORNER BRACES

NAIL & GLUE JOINTS

CORNER DETAIL

SEATING MODULES

Using the diagram *above*, build simple squares with cushions for extra seating or footstools. Add on backs for chairs; group the chairs to make a sofa. As you can see from the drawing, the secret of the soft, squashy look is the wood-box-wrapped-with-foam construction. Choose a loose-weave fabric cover such as Indian cotton. Hand-sew the corners as shown on the base and back. Also cover some 5-inch-thick foam blocks for back pillows on chairs. Just wrap and staple the corners of the seats.

Materials list:
Three 1x12s, 28 inches long
Two 1x12s, 26½ inches long
One piece ¾-inch plywood, 26¼x26¼ inches
Four triangular corner braces, one piece ¾-inch
    plywood, 6x6 inches
Two metal straps, ⅛x2x16 inches
Six yards of 48-inch-wide fabric
One piece of 5-inch high-density foam 26¼x26¼ inches
One piece of 5-inch high-density foam 26x12 inches
2/3 yard 1-inch foam 36 inches wide
Two yards ½-inch foam 36 inches wide

Futons and zabutons are exotic-sounding terms used to describe the furnishings pictured *above*. Actually, they're nothing more than over-stuffed, outsized pillows that can be arranged or stacked in any configuration to suit lounging or sleeping. As their placement here demonstrates, futons and zabutons lend an air of Oriental simplicity that is both casual and elegant. Filled with layers of combed cotton batting, they offer a colorful, comfortable alterna-tive to conventional beds and sofas. What's more, they are inexpensive. You could fill a whole room with futons (the larger pillows) for less than what you'd pay for a single, medium-priced sofa. Futons and zabutons come in a vari-ety of sizes, and their cotton duck covers are available in many pleasing colors.

The simple, block-shaped coffee tables have recessed bases and a laminated finish. They, too, are available in various colors. The smaller bunching table measures 15x15 inches, and the larger is 22x54 inches. The two squat table lamps feature handmade rattan bases.

Sleek elegance (at a reasonable cost) is offered by this sheet-glass dining table with a pair of colorful steel trestles—a nice update on the old sawhorses-under-a-door idea. The table, 28 inches high, is sturdy enough to be used as a work space as well as a dining surface. Also high style and inexpensive are the lightweight, folding metal chairs, available in several glossy colors.

As in the living room, the Oriental mood of the dining area is underscored by the high-shine natural wood floor. The warm brown tones and the beautiful lacquer-like sheen are deceptively simple to achieve: they are the result of two easy-to-apply coats of polyurethane.

Shoji screens contribute greatly to the Far East flavor of the setting. These screens are homemade (with wood laths and translucent paper), but similar screens can be bought ready-made. Place the screens in front of a window, or—as shown here—line them along a wall and light them artificially from behind.

These days, it's possible to spend as much money on a quilt, comforter, or bedspread as on an ordinary mattress! To sidestep high prices, consider making the eye-catching, country-style quilt pictured here. It's a no-sew quilt that you can start in the morning and snuggle under later that night. The time-saver comes from using all-purpose white glue (don't worry, it'll stand up to dry cleaning).

You'll need 6 yards of white felt and 1 yard of blue, or whatever color you prefer. (Both should measure 75 inches wide.)

Cut the white felt into two pieces, each 108 inches long, to fit a double or queen-size bed. From the blue felt, cut 184 3x3-inch squares.

Spread an old sheet on the floor to work on. Lay one sheet of the white felt on top and measure 9½ inches in from each end for a design that measures 56x89 inches overall. Pin several rows of squares in place. Then, using a thin but continuous bead of glue around the edges and an X across the center, stick the squares in place. Press the entire piece with a warm iron and allow it to dry completely and cool. Then loosely roll up the quilt top.

To attach the backing felt to the patched piece, start by drawing parallel lines of glue (like the rules on notebook paper) down from the top of the second piece of white felt. Place the rolled felt on top, unroll about 2 feet, match the edges, and press down. Allow this section to dry before gluing the next 2 feet. Continue this process until the quilt is complete.

Trim the quilt, if necessary, and press with a warm iron.

High-style decorating on a budget adds versatility as well as good looks to this small dining room, *left*.

The key to the room's flexibility lies in the way the end wall has been used for a cantilevered bench. It's made of pine boards painted white and held in place by two wooden braces. The six cushions on the bench are actually bed pillows covered with remnants of colorful chintz fabric. When extra seating is needed, the Parsons-style dining table can be extended and rotated to face the built-in bench (extra leaves, not shown here, will bring the table's length to 120 inches).

The ladder-back chairs, painted to match the white laminate table, were bought as unfinished furniture.

To update the lighting, the central chandelier was removed and three metal industrial lamps were painted yellow and suspended at three different levels at the end of the bench. Additional lighting is provided by a lamp on the sideboard, out of view.

Platform beds, complete with storage drawers, make the most of this tiny, eaved bedroom, *above*. Purchased unfinished, the beds were given a linseed oil finish to bring out the grain while maintaining the natural light color of the wood. Each twin bed is topped with a soft down comforter protected by a removable, washable coverlet sewn from sheets. The toss pillows are stock bed pillows covered in pastel shades of polished cotton.

The luscious orange parfait tone of the comforters is repeated in the rag rug and the old quilt folded at the end of one bed. The same warm color also is used at the room's one window in a pouf shade made from another sheet. The swing-arm lamp provides light for both beds.

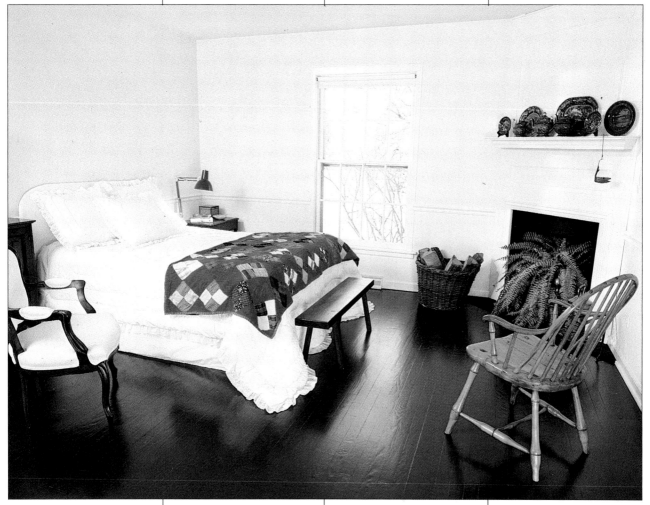

Paint offers a decorative, dollarwise solution to the problem of damaged or badly worn wood floors. Refinishing, of course, offers another solution, but only if the floor deserves the expense and labor involved. The floor in this bedroom, *above,* was not worthy of a refinishing job, but its looks were improved immeasurably by a coat of navy blue paint. To achieve a similar high-gloss effect, use a good-quality enamel paint and seal it with a coat or two of polyurethane. A second option is to use one of the new, tough deck enamels. They come in colors just begging to be brought indoors.

Talk about small space! The nook pictured *at right* measures only 4x5 feet, but some clever handiwork made good use of this smidgen of space. The compact breakfast bar is constructed from 1-inch plywood with a 1x2-inch pine lip. The shelf is faced with orange plastic laminate and is supported by 1x2s screwed into the wall studs at the sides and the back. Extra eye appeal is offered by the glossy green-painted walls.

Casual elegance is the hallmark of the seating group pictured here. The chairs, with their wooden frames and canvas seats and backs, are updated versions of the popular director's chair. The chair backs tilt for added comfort. Placed in the curve of a bay window area, the simple-lined shapes are beautifully silhouetted against the stark white background. Both the chairs and the small snack table fold for easy moving and space-saving storage.

Contributing to this gracious, yet unpretentious, setting is a 4x6-foot rag rug in soft confectionary colors.

It stands to reason that the less furniture you have in a room, the more money you're bound to save. This isn't to suggest that you opt for spartan surroundings simply to cut down on furnishings costs. Quite the contrary. The pared-down look stands on its own as an elegant approach to interior design. The fact that you can save money by creating this look is merely icing on the cake.

chapter

4 Simplicity Saves

It's the quality of the furnishings, not the quantity, that makes this room such a standout. By deliberately limiting the number of furniture pieces to a plump rolled-arm sofa, a matching chaise, and a sleek, black coffee table, the owners have created an eye-catching study in simplicity.

Against a background of stately windows and slate gray walls, the seating arrangement becomes an island of plushness and comfort. The minimalist approach succeeds in enhancing the visual impact of both the furniture and the vintage architecture that embraces it.

Contemporary finishes, colors, and materials bring the old architecture up to date. The windows and floor are particularly noteworthy. Stripped of its old finish, the cypress woodwork looks elegant with just a coating of beeswax. And the pine floor, sanded down and refinished with ebony stain and an application of glossy urethane, is spectacular.

Totally devoid of excess furnishings and frills, this clear-the-deck decorating scheme is pleasingly restful and soothing to the eye. Part of the room's beauty comes from the background that's as natural and unadorned as the furniture. Soft off-white covers the walls; the floor is painted with white deck paint.

Seating couldn't be simpler (or less costly). Four large floor pillows, covered to match the window seat cushions, line up on a natural sisal rug. The contemporary, low-profile coffee table is actually a wooden skid purchased from a warehouse.

The window area was converted into a comfortable sofa substitute by building in a seating platform topped with a canvas-covered foam slab.

Recessed niches flanking the window have been turned into showcases for accessories, and out-of-the-way compartments for stereo speakers. The speakers are placed at the top of each niche, and are concealed by a facade of 1x2s spaced one inch apart. Similar screening below camouflages an old radiator and a storage cupboard. The screening also serves to maintain the trim, architectural look of the room.

In the niches themselves, twin arrangements of dried weeds provide dramatic impact for little cost. As a general rule, accessories are more effective when limited in number—especially in a simple setting like this one. (A miscellany of small accessories is apt to come across as clutter.)

Custom may dictate that a living room be furnished with at least one sofa, but often it pays (in more ways than one) to ignore convention and play by your own rules instead. The living room at *right* is a case in point. Two beautifully contoured armless chairs take the place of a standard sofa, but with no loss to the look and comfort of the room. When the chairs aren't providing cozy fireside seating, they can be pushed together or moved about as needed. The small cube coffee table also is easily moved to accommodate the placement of the chairs. What's nice about modular furnishings like these is that you can buy just a few pieces to suit your needs and your pocketbook, then add other furnishings later.

When decorating a room from scratch, is it better to buy one fine item with the money at hand or to stretch your dollars to buy as many furnishings as possible? Our suggestion—if it comes down to making a choice—is to opt for one fine piece that you're sure to love for years to come and fill in the gaps with less expensive "interim" pieces. In the long run you'll be much happier with this approach. True, it takes patience to decorate over a period of time, but all in all, the end result is worth the wait.

In this dining room, *left*, a magnificent rosewood table is the unquestionable star of the show. Though relatively expensive, it was chosen to provide a lifetime of classic beauty and practical function. The contemporary fold-up metal chairs provide inexpensive but handsome interim seating pieces.

Simplified decorating can help you save space as well as money. This small, 13x16-foot bedroom acquired lots of needed storage with little loss of floor space simply by adding a built-in closet on both sides of the bed. The closets are fitted with drawers, thus eliminating the need for dressers.

Floor-to-ceiling doors with magnetic catches instead of knobs make the storage closets appear to blend into the wall. An upholstered panel stretching between the closets forms the headboard. Teak nightstands fit neatly beneath the horizontal panel on both sides of the bed.

To create the look of a platform bed, the ordinary Hollywood frame (on casters) was encased with a wood panel frame, and—for a unifying effect—covered with a remnant of grey, flat-woven carpet to match the floor.

The tailored, white cotton bedspread was given a classy, custom look by sewing a handsome weaving into the center of the spread. The woven piece adds an exotic touch of color to the other-wise neutral scheme.

The simple window treat-ment also contributes to the architectural look of the room. It consists of a solid-color Roman shade hung at ceiling height and framed by vertical 1x2s.

The stripped-down look offers yet another benefit: it saves time. With less furniture and fewer accessories to gath-er dust, you'll spend less time on housecleaning.

This ultra-serene, all-white bedroom, *right,* is practically maintenance-free. The uphol-stered "island" bed sits on casters and is easily moved for floor sweeping. The ce-ramic tile floor requires only an occasional damp-mopping.

Bedmaking, too, is a breeze. In lieu of a top sheet and blankets, a duvet (Euro-pean-style comforter) is used instead. By adopting this kind of sleep style, you really don't need to make the bed at all. Upon arising, you merely stow the duvet in a closet or fold it at the foot of the bed.

One Room Four Ways

chapter

5

Redecorating a room can be an expensive proposition, but there is one way to save money. The secret, as you'll see on the next six pages, is to make the most of color. By taking full advantage of this powerful decorating tool, you can completely change the appearance of a room—any room—without spending a small fortune on new furnishings. To show you how it's done, we've taken a 15x18-foot living room and given it four distinctly different looks just by changing the color scheme with fabrics, accents, and paint.

To prove the power of color, we first put together a neutral scheme that's as low-key and livable as a room can be. Because all the hues are on the quiet side, there are no strident notes to jar the eye or the psyche. But don't be fooled into thinking of the neutrals as no-colors. Beige, brown, gray, black, and white are pleasing colors in their own right, not just foils for more vibrant hues.

To keep a room like this one, *left,* from becoming too quiescent, it's necessary to call on an interplay of textures. Applying the old rule about including surfaces that are rough, smooth, shiny, and dull works to perfection here. The matte finish of the almond-colored walls plays up the shine of the lacquered Parsons-style coffee table, the polished drum table, and the ceramic and brass lamps. The nubby textures of the upholstery fabric and the large area rug contrast beautifully with the wide-plank pine floor.

Both the chaise longue and the sofa are flexible, modular pieces that can be moved around to form various configurations. Thus, not only can the room's color scheme be easily changed, but the seating arrangement can be as well.

Simple matchstick blinds filter light at the windows and are perfect adjuncts to the neutral, understated setting.

How to Change the
SCENE
with
FABRIC

This is the same room you saw on the two previous pages, but its character has been changed considerably. The basic elements—walls, floor, and the major furnishings—remain the same, but the overall look is altogether different. The color coup comes from the introduction of a pastel print fabric. Used as a slipcover on the chaise longue, the floral print serves as a decorative springboard for other color additions to the room.

A handsome dhurrie rug in melon tones replaces the nubby, neutral one. The new rug adds subtle pattern and texture underfoot and blends nicely with the mellow wood floor. (Dhurries are available in a wide variety of colors, pattern designs, and price ranges. The least expensive dhurries are made of cotton; the most costly are those made of wool.)

The almond-hued matchstick blinds are holdovers from the first scheme. They've been softened with shirred drapery side panels and fabric-covered rods in a blue-green hue picked up from the slipcover. The flowing panels add a touch of tra-

ditional styling to the room. Other traditional elements are the black-shaded floor lamp, the vase-shaped table lamp, and the precision lineup of framed floral prints on the sofa wall.

There are several other small, but effective, decorative touches worth noting here. One is the use of a tall, leafy plant. Not only does it "furnish" an empty corner, but lighted from below with a canister lamp, it adds an aura of drama to the setting. To help balance color and pattern throughout the room, two large sofa pillows were covered with remnants of the slipcover fabric. The smaller toss pillows were covered with chintz and loosely filled for a squashy look.

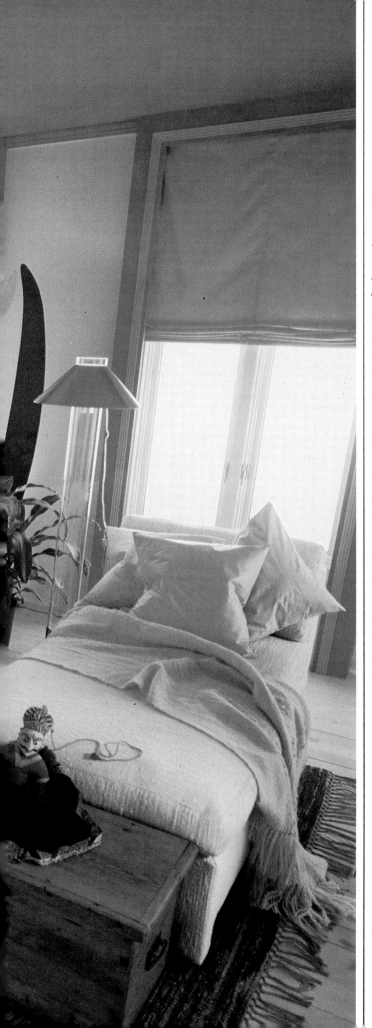

How to Change the
SCENE
with
ACCENTS

This not-for-the-faint-hearted change of scene got its inspiration from the framed print hanging over the sofa. Here again, the furnishings stay the same; it's the spirited infusion of color and artful accents that gives this room its lively new look.

First, watermelon pink was chosen from the serendipitous mix of colors in the print. Used on the ceiling, the effect is striking and unconventional. Draperies and blinds have disappeared from the windows; in their place are narrow lambrequins painted pink to match the ceiling and trimmed in gold. The coordinating Roman shades are made of shiny chintz fabric.

The colorful collection of accessories underscores the lighthearted scheme. Conversation-piece art is provided by a freestanding abstract flower sculpture on the window wall. A pair of floor lamps with see-through acrylic bases and metal shades appear as if they're floating on air.

Anchoring the compact seating group is a handmade rag rug in shades of pink and blue. Its darker color helps balance the impact of the vibrant pink ceiling.

Track lights are a notable addition to this easy-to-change-and-rearrange room. Two of the light canisters are beamed on the artwork; the others shed light on the pedestaled plant.

A lesson to be learned from this room scheme is that accents—be they in the form of artwork, accessories, or color—can be used to spice up an outdated decorating scheme, or to inspire a colorful new one. Remember: By starting with clean-lined, classic furnishings, you can steer a room in almost any direction you want.

How to Change the
SCENE
with
PAINT

Here's a striking example of what color can do to completely transform the look of a room. Now sleek and ultra-sophisticated, the room bears little resemblance to the original play-it-safe scheme (pages 42-43). The agent of change, quite obviously, is paint. Warm, cocoa brown envelops the room and provides a splendid, contrasting background for the furnishings. To keep this authoritative hue from overpowering the room, the ceiling and the trim are painted white.

Walls aren't the only places where paint can work its decorating magic. Here the once-white coffee table gets a new look with several coats of cotton-candy-pink paint. Even the distinctive floral designs on the sofa pillows were created with spray paint and cardboard stencils. And the artwork that wraps around one corner of the room is an original paint-on-fabric creation by artist Carolyn Ray.

The random-plank flooring has been brushed with high-gloss polyurethane to give it a sleek wet look. The shiny sealer also serves to accentuate the beauty of the wood.

No safari is necessary to obtain a "zebra" rug like the one shown here. You can make one yourself with a piece of canvas and a can of paint. Simply cut standard artist's canvas to shape, then add stripes with brown acrylic paint. To protect your handiwork from dirt and dust, seal the surface (after the paint has completely dried) with a coat of polyurethane.

Here again, track lighting is used to highlight the art wall and provide a sense of drama. A paper light sculpture adds yet another element of interest to this exciting, contemporary setting.

Smart Solutions

chapter **6**

It is one thing to fill a room with furniture, but it's quite another to unify the various visual elements into a pleasing, cohesive whole. The walls, windows, floor, ceiling, *and* furniture are all part of the total picture, and must be dealt with as such. In this chapter we will show you a variety of decorative devices to help you add the harmony and style that give a room its "put together" appeal.

This cozy, under-the-eaves sitting room, *left and above,* is simply furnished but filled with flair. The secret of the successful scheme lies in the clever coordination of color and pattern.

Almost everything you see in the room—the upholstery fabric, the curtains, the table skirts, the wallpaper, even the paint—is from a special pre-matched collection of fabrics and wall coverings. Designed to take the guesswork out of mixing and matching, the collections are a boon for the novice decorator. All you have to do is pick one basic pattern as your starting point, then supplement with other coordinating prints.

Nothing can take the place of color for giving a small room a sense of style. In this compact living/dining area, *opposite page,* a primary color scheme adds lots of oomph to the otherwise simple, unpretentious setting. The cheery red, yellow, and blue combination gives the room a refreshing visual and psychological lift.

Although a primary color scheme is one of the easiest to work with, there are some "rules" to remember, nevertheless. First, avoid using equal amounts of all three colors; instead, pick one color as the dominant hue. Here,

blue is used as the base color; red and yellow are used sparingly as small, but effective, accents. Second, don't go overboard with primaries. The most successful schemes are those that are tempered with white, neutrals, or both.

The perky primary color scheme is carried over to the compact dining area, *above.* Here, however, red is used as the dominant color, with blue napkins serving as eye-catching accents.

To visually separate the dining area from the rest of the room, the wall is papered instead of painted. A natural pine trestle table and four

canvas-seat director's chairs offer a lot of style and function for a relatively small amount of money. When needed, the chairs double as extra seating in the living area. The table, too, functions in more ways than one. During parties, it is pushed up against the wall and used as a buffet. At other times, it does duty as a desk, a game table, and a handy work surface for sewing and crafts projects.

Lighting is what gives this room its special glow. And even if your do-it-yourself skills are limited, you can create similar effects. The fixture over the dining table is a replacement for an outdated hanging lamp. The new fixture consists of a simple plug strip screwed into the ceiling, and a piece of painted wood suspended from the strip. Clamped to the wood piece are three inexpensive spotlights with meant-to-be-seen curly white cords. No special wiring is involved; the cords are simply plugged into the already-wired ceiling strip.

On the adjacent wall, an energy-saving wash of light gives the room its overall warmth. Easy-to-make, three-sided wooden columns conceal the light source: new warm-hued fluorescent plug-in tubes that bounce light on the shelves and into the rest of the room.

It's hard to believe that not too long ago this house, *left and above,* was a 1950s has-been. With nothing more than an influx of new finishes and slick, contemporary furnishings, the once-dowdy dwelling is now wonderfully in step with today.

The transformation began with liberal applications of white paint on just about everything—walls, ceilings, doors, and woodwork. Then came white vertical blinds to slick up the old-style windows. Together with the white walls, ceiling, and moderately-priced modular furniture, the window treatment contributes beautifully to the flow of space and light.

Completing the update is an off-white ceramic tile floor.

Though not inexpensive, the floor is an elegant addition to the room. A similar look could be achieved (at considerably less cost) with vinyl resilient flooring designed to look like ceramic tile.

The small dining alcove (located just behind the modular seating units) has been given a spacious look with the addition of a mirrored wall above the built-in storage unit/buffet. The Parsons-style dining table was purchased in an unfinished state, then sheathed with sleek white plastic laminate.

Here again, white vertical blinds have been used. Note how they disguise the small, squat windows and create a space-expanding "window wall" effect.

Budget Brighteners

chapter

7

Rarely used guest rooms and other "spare" spaces have a tendency to turn into unsightly catchalls for household clutter. Such was the state of this small room, *left*, before it was decoratively and functionally refurbished.

The first order of business was to create extra storage by building narrow cabinets on each side of the window. The cabinet doors, with their exposed hinges, consist of natural-finish pine boards nailed to two crosspieces.

A wooden sawhorse-door combination provides a large work surface at a low price. Painted glossy red, the desk has a slick uptown look.

Scalloped café curtains hung low on the window camouflage the wall below. A shade covered in matching fabric (not shown) completes the attractive treatment. Additional decorative dash is provided by the striped cotton dhurrie rug.

In this chapter you will find a variety of ideas to help you enliven a lackluster room. None of the projects is major in terms of time, talent, or financial expenditure required. Indeed, all of the room-brightening ideas are easy on the pocketbook and most can be accomplished in a weekend or less.

If your kitchen is looking dated and dingy, take heart. There *are* ways to effect a face-lift without spending large sums of money. The clever solution for the kitchen *above* was to first paint the dark wood cupboards white, then add an eye-catching "tile" treatment.

Although the tiles look like the costly ceramic kind, they're actually inexpensive dimestore decals applied to pieces of painted hardboard. The photos *at left* show what an easy project this is. Note: Be sure to let the paint dry before applying the decals.

Here's another decorative idea for a kitchen in need of improvement. The original cabinets, though fairly new, were rather plain and ordinary in appearance. Now, with the help of flowers cut from self-adhesive plastic, the cupboards are abloom with color and interest. To create a similar treatment, use a pencil or chalk to mark the doors, drawers, and other surfaces with a 4½-inch-square grid pattern. Once the pattern is complete, apply thin strips of tape over the pencil lines. Use the patterns provided *at right* to make the flower cutouts.

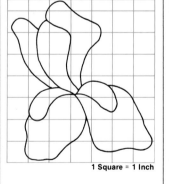

1 Square = 1 Inch

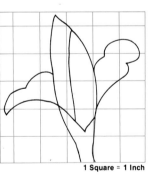

1 Square = 1 Inch

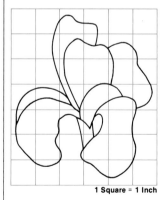

1 Square = 1 Inch

This pretty and practical braided rug is put together with flannel bed sheets. To make your own 62-inch-round rug, you'll need six flannel sheets (twin size, extra long) in pastel colors of your choice, heavy-duty thread, and a needle.

Just follow these how-to instructions: First, cut the sheets into 2½-inch strips; sew strips together end-to-end. Next, fold the raw edges to the inside so the strip is 2 inches wide. Fold the strip in half lengthwise so that it measures 1 inch wide.

Pin the ends of three different color strips together and begin the braiding process. Add strips as necessary. Working on a flat surface, slip-stitch the braid into a flat coil with heavy-duty thread. Be careful to avoid stretching the braid as you sew. Ease to allow sufficient fullness on the outside of the braid so the rug lies flat.

A fanciful painted floor treatment turned this nursery, *right,* into a colorful land of enchantment. The whimsical creatures residing in the painted tree are enlarged adaptations of the wallpaper motif. The floor design was drawn freehand, then painted with bright shades of oil-base enamel. Several coats of clear polyurethane protect the painted surface.

If freehand drawing is not your forte, consider having a photographic blowup made of a favorite wallpaper pattern, then make cutouts and trace them onto the floor.

Here are two small paint projects that promise quick, but effective, results. Bright stripes of deck enamel add lots of personality to this pint-size pantry, *left.* For best results, work with one color at a time, and let the paint dry completely before going on to the next color.

A stippled effect was employed to give decorative punch to the mundane industrial metal shelf unit. The technique is quite simple. First give the shelves a coat of white enamel. Then, after the paint has dried, use a sponge to dab small amounts of green paint (or any color you choose) in a random pattern. Too much paint on the sponge will cause smearing. To avoid this problem, pat the sponge on a piece of cardboard (before you start stippling the shelves) to remove excess paint.

Vintage bathrooms can be very charming, but their color schemes are often passé. Such was the case in the bathroom *at left*. The original color of the tiles, tub, sink, and toilet was a rather unappealing shade of pink. Now, with the application of several coats of epoxy paint, all traces of pink have been banished. Practical as it is for updating an old bathroom, epoxy is rather difficult to work with. Proper surface preparation is essential to the success of painting with epoxy, so be sure to carefully read the directions on the can before you begin.

Guests who visit this bathroom, *right,* can't help but crack a smile when they see this whimsical paintbrush "put-on." Sketched and painted freehand on a blank wall, the imaginary window with its impish "peeping Toms" (and Tinas) is a just-for-fun decorating project.

For a simpler *trompe l'oeil* effect, try your hand at an outdoor scene with a painted-on half-raised window.

A new small-print wallpaper and matching fabric gave this 1950s bathroom a decorative shot in the arm. The fabric was used to create a skirted camouflage for the exposed fixtures under the sink.

The softly shirred skirt is attached to the lavatory with Velcro fasteners. The hard side of the fastener is glued to the sink edge; the soft side is stitched to the back of the skirt ½ inch from the top, allowing the heading to stand free. The camel-colored trim and matching bows repeat the color of the clover pattern in the wallpaper and fabric.

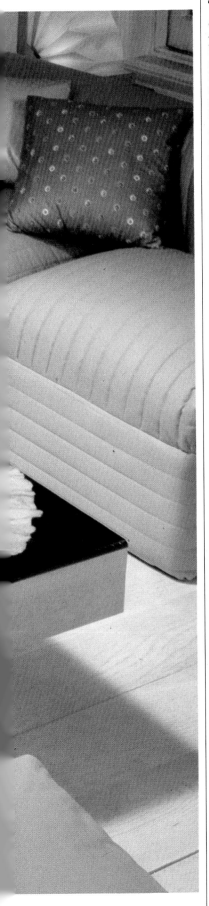

This unusual, *eye-catching* coffee table, *left,* features a 40x43-inch photographic blowup of a flower. You can create a similar tabletop by having a photo lab enlarge and custom box mount your favorite photograph on hardboard. Standard box mounts are 2 inches deep; this one is 6 inches deep to obscure a clear view of the light underneath. The base for this table consists of eight 8x8x4-inch glass bricks from a building supply store. Arrange the bricks in a square, standing them on their sides so there's a space in the center for a porcelain light fixture fitted with a 60- or 75-watt bulb. Use epoxy to glue the bricks together; let them stand (about 10 hours) until the adhesive has set. Screw a light socket to the underside of the tabletop, or set it on a wood block on the floor. The box rests on the table base; its weight is enough to keep the table steady. To protect the photo, have a sheet of glass cut to fit the top.

A solid-mirrored wall can be very elegant, but also quite expensive. A handsome and effective alternative is a wall lined with full-length mirror panels from a variety or discount store. The least-costly panels come with unfinished wooden frames. Depending on your decor, you can hang the frames in their unfinished state, or paint or stain them the color of your choice. Use plastic wall anchors to mount the mirrors on the wall.

chapter 8
Crafty Ideas

Consider yourself fortunate if you enjoy working on crafts projects and other handiwork items. Not only do crafts offer a pleasurable, relaxing pastime, but the finished projects—be they decorative or utilitarian—can add greatly to the charm and personality of your home.

Once looked down upon as a poor man's floor covering, rag rugs today are much in demand. Collectors seek them as examples of American folk art; non-collectors admire them for their wonderful colors and decorative appeal. However, as with most things that are highly sought after, prized rag rugs have become quite costly.

Pictured here is a delightful rag rug that needn't cost you a *sou*. It's a homemade version that's created with a colorful assortment of recycled materials—old draperies, tablecloths, bedspreads, bath towels, flannel bathrobes, slacks, skirts, shirts, and other rag bag items. The materials are cut and sewn into long strips, then woven—potholder fashion—on a large make-it-yourself loom. How-to directions begin on page 70.

1. Follow these directions to make your own rag rug. Tear (or cut) fabrics into 4- or 5-inch-wide strips. In all, you'll need about 50 yards of 45-inch-wide fabric. Half of the strips should be non-stretchy fabrics such as cotton or corduroy. These will make the "warp"—the strips that make a base to weave through. The other strips (the ones for weaving) should be stretch fabrics such as nylon, double knits, or jersey.

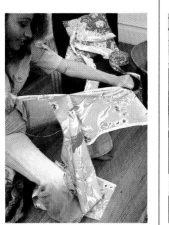

2. Sew and roll the fabric strips until you have enough to make a rug. To make the strips easier to handle, sew them together into 8- to 10-yard lengths. Roll up the strips as you go along, folding under the edges. You'll need about thirty 10-foot-long rolls of stretchy fabric and thirty-five 8-foot-long rolls of sturdier fabric. It's best to have all the strips rolled and ready to go before you begin to weave.

3. Building the loom: The only tools you'll need are a screwdriver, a tape measure, and a hammer.

Here's the shopping list for materials needed to build your loom:
• Four 6-foot 2x2s
• 300 3-inch finish nails (get some extras in case you bend a few)
• Eight 3-inch wood screws
• Four 6-inch corner braces (with 1¼-inch wood screws)

First screw together the 2x2s into a square; then reinforce the corners with braces, as shown *below*. Mark off each inch (72 per board) with a pencil. Drive nails into the marks, about one inch deep.

4. Once the frame is ready, you can begin to weave. First, warp the loom with sturdy fabrics. Tie the end of the first roll of fabric (pick one that doesn't ravel easily) to a corner nail. Then loop the fabric, going back and forth around each nail, sewing on each new strip as you need it. (Be sure the raw edges are turned under.) One important rule: *Don't* pull the fabric too tight—it should be slack enough to lie along the floor. Also, keep your eye on the rug as a whole: The warp is the pattern of the rug, so plan the colors and textures before you begin.

3 INCH WOOD SCREWS

REINFORCE WITH CORNER BRACES

2×2's

Rag Rug Tips

- Choose colorful fabrics for your rug—the brighter the colors, the better.
- Corduroy and velveteen tear easily into strips and add texture to the rug.
- Electric scissors will make the strip cutting much easier.
- If you'd rather use new material, you'll need about 50 yards of 45-inch-wide fabric (for the sturdy and stretchy fabrics combined).
- Build the loom in the room where you'll be weaving. A 6x6-foot loom with 288 nails sticking out can be very awkward to move.
- Tuck the fabric edges under as you weave—to keep them from raveling.
- If the rug pulls too tightly on the loom as you weave the last few rows, simply bend the nails a bit to ease the strain.
- For best results, limit the size of your rag rug to 6x6 feet (a loom much larger than this is just too unwieldy). Smaller dimensions will work, however, such as 7x3 feet for a hall runner.
- To make a rectangular rug, warp the width and weave the length.

5. It gets a bit tricky when you start weaving because the stretchy strips are doubled as they go through. Lay an unrolled strip of stretchy fabric across the loom, as pictured *above,* grabbing it a few inches beyond the edge of the loom (you've measured your first double strip to weave with). Hang onto this loop and take the strip back to the other side; start weaving. Hook the loop on the nail when you finish each row, then measure and weave again. Sew on new rolls as you need them. If a row bulges too much in the middle, skip a nail on each side.

6. Finish off the edges with a series of loops. Unfasten a loop from one of the corner nails; tie or sew the end of a stretchy fabric strip to the loop. Using a crochet stitch, take off one loop at a time, pushing the edging strip through this loop to make a new loop. Make another loop in the edging strip and push it through the loop just made. Continue around the rug.

Batik—a distinctive method of hand-printing textiles with wax and dyes—offers many decorative applications for the home. By mastering basic batik techniques, you can create a setting as cheery and colorful as this one.

Inspiration for the batik designs shown here comes from Henri Matisse's painting, "The Purple Robe" (a framed print of this work hangs on the wall). The pillows, seat cushions, curtains, tablecloth, and floor covering are all homemade batik creations that you can make in a few weekends' time.

If you'd like to learn more about the Indonesian art of batik, just turn the page. We've included simple how-to instructions for many of the projects pictured here.

BATIK

For projects shown on pages 72-73, you will need the materials and tools listed below. Read all the instructions, *general* and *specific*, before you begin.

GENERAL INSTRUCTIONS

The materials you'll need are:
• Men's white, 100-percent-cotton hankies or white, unsized, 45-inch-wide, 100-percent-cotton fabric (available in quiltmakers' supply stores or batik art supply stores), or old, well-washed 100-percent-cotton sheets (see "Precautions," *right*).
• Procion or high-intensity, cold-water fabric dyes (available in art and crafts stores) in the following colors: lemon yellow, gold-yellow, fuchsia, red-orange, red, light blue, turquoise, forest green, black.
• Beeswax and paraffin wax; pickling or table salt; sodium alginate or a batik dye thickening agent, such as Hi-Dye Print Base; Arm and Hammer Super Washing Soda Detergent Booster or other salt soda; baking soda; water softener.

You'll also need the following tools: a kitchen blender or wire whip (for mixing the thickener); an electric frying pan and a pie tin with wire; tinfoil (or substitute a small pan set in water for the pie tin, frying pan, and tinfoil); pencil; watercolor brushes; waxing brush; protective gloves; 3- to 4-gallon enameled, stainless steel, glass, or plastic dyebath container; 3- to 4-gallon kettle (for boiling out wax); glass or plastic measuring cup and some type of stirring stick (spoon or wooden dowel); plastic bags (for curing); paper towels; newspapers; cleansing bleach (for cleanup); apron; small glass or plastic lidded containers (for storing dyes); and stretching frame or embroidery hoop.

PRECAUTIONS

As with any activity involving the use of chemicals or other potentially harmful materials or procedures, you must plan carefully before you begin and take safety precautions while you are working. Batik involves using hot wax, so DO NOT LEAVE children unattended in your work area. And do not leave the work area while wax is melting in the pan. Keep baking soda handy to douse an electrical fire. Work in a well-ventilated, well-illuminated area. If you observe the following precautions, you should find batik a rewarding experience.

DO NOT WORK in a food preparation area; the dyes are contaminating. Reserve tools (except blender, wire whip, and frying pan) for batiking only. DO NOT RETURN batik pans to the kitchen. DO NOT USE aluminum, copper, or galvanized pans for batik.

For large projects, wear a face mask to avoid breathing contaminating dye particles. Wear rubber gloves to avoid staining your skin.

When purchasing materials for batik, DO NOT substitute cotton/polyester fabric blends or hot-water dyes for materials listed at left if you wish to duplicate bright colors. Synthetic fabrics resist dyes, and hot-water dyes will destroy wax lines.

PREPARING THE FABRIC

To make the fabric more receptive to dye, soak it in a soda bath first. Mix ½ cup washing soda in a quart of hot water until dissolved. Pour the liquid into a soaking tub, add 3 quarts of cold water, and stir. Soak the fabric in liquid for 15 minutes, then hang the fabric to dry. To smooth the fabric, steam-press with an iron set at the "wool" or "low" setting.

DRAWING AND PAINTING THE DESIGN

Lightly draw the design onto the fabric with a pencil. Mount the fabric in a large embroidery hoop or on an artist's stretching frame. This makes the fabric easier to paint and wax.

To paint the design on the fabric (see photo 1), you'll need a thickening agent to combine with the dyes. This will make the dye "paintable."

Use a purchased thickener for batik or mix your own. To mix a thickening agent, pour 1 quart water into a blender; sprinkle 2 tablespoons of sodium alginate into the water; blend to a smooth consistency like that of heavy cream. Pour the contents into a glass jar; cover and store until needed. *Note:* The thickener is not a contaminant and can be mixed safely in a blender used to prepare food.

To prepare dye for painting in the design, mix 1 teaspoon of dye to 1 cup of thickener in a small lidded container. (For small projects, mix ¼ teaspoon dye to ¼ cup of thickener.) Add a pinch of baking soda to the mix to activate the dye.

With watercolor brushes, paint in parts of the design (see specific instructions, *opposite*), blotting off excess dye with paper toweling to keep thickened dye from running while drying. Air-dry the painted fabric. Rinse the painted fabric with cold water to remove any excess color and to set color. Gradually increase the temperature of the water to warm until the rinse water is clear. Air-dry again.

WAXING THE DESIGN TO RESIST DYE

If you want the batik to have a smooth appearance, use a soft wax combination of 1 part beeswax to 3 parts paraffin wax. For a more crackled look, use paraffin wax only.

Prepare a pan for melting the wax by lining an electric frypan with tinfoil (to catch wax drips). Set a metal pie tin on the tinfoil and fasten a wire snugly across the pie tin and around the frying pan, firmly twisting wire ends together. Use the wire to wipe excess wax from the brush during waxing. Heat the wax in the pie tin to 275 degrees Fahrenheit; turn the dial down when the wax is hot enough and reheat the wax when it cools.

Caution: *DO NOT LEAVE hot wax unattended. DO NOT ALLOW wax to overheat. Be sure not to spill wax on the electric coils of the heating unit. Hot wax is flammable. DO NOT try to put out a wax fire with water; extinguish the fire with baking soda or invert a large pot over the flame to cut off oxygen to the fire.*

With a brush used only for wax, cover the painted areas of the design with wax (see photo 2); cover all parts of the unpainted fabric that should remain white. The waxing step fills in the fibers of the fabric and keeps the dye from penetrating during the dipping step. Only the unwaxed sections of the fabric will accept dye.

DIPPING THE DESIGN IN DYE

To prepare the dyebath (see photo 3), put 1 teaspoon of dye, 1 tablespoon of water softener, 1 cup salt, and 2 gallons of 90-degree water in the dyebath container. Stir well and immerse painted/waxed fabric in dyebath. Stir for 10 minutes; remove the fabric, add 1½ teaspoons washing soda (dissolved in hot water before adding to dyebath), and return fabric to the tub. Stir occasionally for 15 minutes.

Note: This mix contains enough dye to dye 2 yards of fabric a medium color. Use smaller amounts of water and dye for smaller projects.

Decrease the amount of water to make the dye stronger. The fabric will appear darker when wet.

Remove the fabric, pressing away excess dye with your hands. Fold the fabric and place it in a plastic bag, pushing the air out of the bag. Tie the bag tightly and let the fabric set for 2 hours.

Rinse the fabric in cool water until the water runs clear; air-dry the fabric.

REMOVING THE WAX FROM FABRIC

Boil water in a nonfood kettle, adding ½ cup of soap flakes or granulated soap. Add the fabric to boiling water; boil for 5 to 10 minutes. Remove the fabric from the boiling water, skimming the wax away from the top of the kettle. Rinse the fabric in clear water to remove more wax. *DO NOT* pour out the kettle over a drain; the wax

will clog the drain. Skim the wax off the top of the cooled water in the kettle before repeating the boiling procedure. (You may need to remove more wax.) Air-dry the fabric. Wash the fabric in the machine; air-dry and press.

PILLOW HOW-TO INSTRUCTIONS

For each pillow, you will need one 16-inch-square, white cotton men's handkerchief, or other white cotton fabric square; one 16-inch fabric square (pillow backing); 2 yards of black piping; 1 lb. polyester fiberfill; thread; batik materials and tools (see "General Instructions," *opposite*); butcher paper.

Enlarge the patterns provided here onto butcher paper. Follow the batik steps, painting the black areas on the patterns with the colors listed below, waxing the painted and white areas and dyeing the gray areas in the colors also listed below.

PILLOW A

1 Square = 2 Inches

Pillow A:
Paint the black areas black; dip the waxed fabric in a pale turquoise dyebath.

PILLOW B

1 Square = 2 Inches

Pillow B:
Paint the leaves yellow-green (combine yellow and green dyes) and the flower centers black. Paint the petals on the small flower yellow, and the petals on the large flower fuchsia. Dip the waxed fabric in purple dye (obtained by combining equal parts of red and blue dyes).

PILLOW C

1 Square = 2 Inches

Pillow C:
Paint the black areas black; dip the waxed fabric in pale turquoise dye.

FINISHING THE PILLOWS

After completing the dyeing process, sew black piping along the raw edges of the pillow front. With right sides facing, sew the pillow back to the pillow front along the previous stitch line. Leave an opening for turning. Turn the pillow right side out, stuff with fiberfill, and sew the pillow closed.

TABLECLOTH HOW-TO

To create the striped tablecloth, mark 1½-inch-wide stripes lengthwise on two 86-inch strips of 45-inch-wide cotton fabric. Wax every other stripe. Dip the waxed fabric in the purple dyebath (refer to the "General Instructions").

When all of the batik steps have been completed, sew the two strips of fabric together with the right sides facing. Press the seam open and hem the tablecloth edges.

CURTAIN

1 Square = 5 Inches

CURTAIN HOW-TO

The colorful curtain panels require 5 yards of 45-inch-wide, white cotton fabric, and batik materials and tools listed in "General Instructions."

Cut or tear the length of fabric into 3 strips: one 11 inches wide, one 28½ inches wide, and another one 5½ inches wide.

Enlarge the pattern shown here onto butcher paper. Repeat the pattern as you work the length of the panels.

Follow the batik steps in "General Instructions." For the wide strip, combine red and green dye to make gray dye. Use a small amount of gray to color the thickener for painting. Paint gray on the areas shown in black on the pattern. Wax the painted areas and dip the fabric strip in dark gray dyebath. (Use gray dye with a little black dye.)

For the medium-wide strip, dip the fabric in turquoise dyebath *first*. Paint the black design on the fabric with black thickened dye. No wax is used on this strip.

For the narrow strip, paint zigzag shapes in lemon yellow. Wax over the yellow areas and dip the strip in red dyebath.

When the batik strips are completed, cut the strips in half crosswise (one for each side of the window).

For each side, sew strips together using ½-inch seam allowances. (See the pattern for the order.) Be sure to reverse the strip order for one side to make matching panels. Hem all the raw edges, fold the curtain tops over 4 inches, and sew along the edges to make rod carriers.

Embroidery floss and a length of fabric are the only materials you need to create this fool-the-eye Austrian shade for your home. The delicate flowers, fringe, and curtain "creases" give the illusion of an intricate, high-priced window treatment, but this one-stitch shade is surprisingly low-cost and easy to make. It requires a minimum of fabric and is worked in one simple embroidery stitch.

The finished size of the Austrian-style shade is 45x67 inches. To make the shade, you'll need the following materials:

• Two yards of 45-inch-wide sheer fabric.

• Two skeins each of dark green, light pink, rose, and magenta embroidery floss.

• Eight skeins of gray embroidery floss.

• Dressmaker's transfer pen or washable marking pen.

• Butcher paper.

• 19x24-inch tissue paper.

How-to is provided on the opposite page.

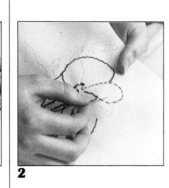

1

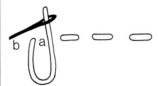

2

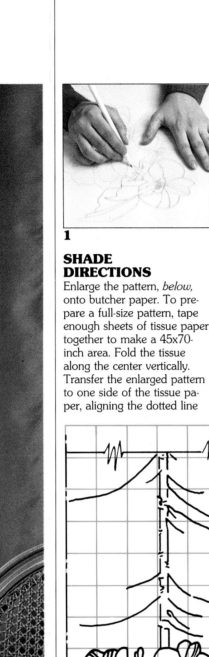

SHADE DIRECTIONS

Enlarge the pattern, *below,* onto butcher paper. To prepare a full-size pattern, tape enough sheets of tissue paper together to make a 45x70-inch area. Fold the tissue along the center vertically. Transfer the enlarged pattern to one side of the tissue paper, aligning the dotted line with the center fold. After drawing one side, fold the tissue paper along the fold; trace over the pattern again to fill out the other side of the design. Slip the tissue

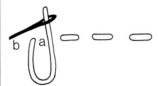

drawing under the curtain fabric; center the design so that you have about 4-inch margins on the selvage edges and about 10 inches of extra fabric at the bottom below the fringe.

Using the transfer pen, trace the design onto the fabric (see photo 1, *above*).

To embroider a line, gently sew running stitches along a line to a turning point; reverse the direction and thread the floss back through each running stitch until you reach the point at which you began. Repeat the stitching procedure for each line, changing colors as needed. See photo 2, *above,* for stitching how-to. Stitch shade lines (creases) in gray; stitch leaves and stems in green. Interchange the three pink shades of floss on the fringe and flowers.

Note: Do not use an embroidery hoop and avoid pulling the threads too taut. Be sure to tie neat knots on the wrong side of the shade; the sheer fabric will not conceal oversize knots.

Machine-stitch a casing at the top and bottom of the shade. Place a curtain rod through the top casing; insert a second rod in the lower casing to keep the shade flat against the window frame.

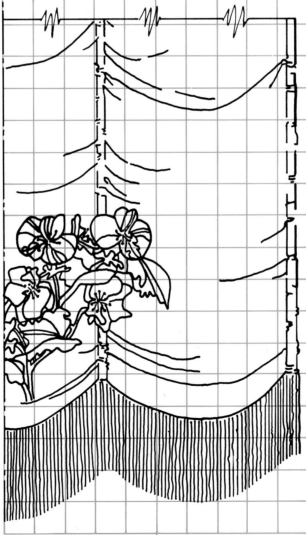

Here's a crafts project that's likely to become a keepsake. Designed for a child, it's an unfinished chest of drawers that's been personalized with a wood chisel and some artists' oil paints.

If you'd like to make a similar chest for a favorite youngster in your life, just follow the steps below and the more detailed instructions on the opposite page.

1. First transfer the drawer motifs to the raw wood surface. Using a sheet of carbon paper, trace over the design lines with a ball-point pen or a pencil tip. Carve away the recessed areas with a wood chisel.

2. Apply a coating of wood stain to the surface of the drawer front. Be sure to fill in the just-carved areas with stain, too.

3. Brush a mixture of artists' oil paints and linseed oil onto both the carved and uncarved areas of the chest.

4. Finish with a coat of spray varnish. If you're new to wood carving, you might try the technique on the lid of a small wooden chest or toy box before tackling a large-scale project like this one.

1

2

3

4

TOP DRAWER

MIDDLE DRAWER

(Put Name Here)

BOTTOM DRAWER

1 Square = 1 inch

CARVED CHEST

MATERIALS NEEDED:
One 28x26x15-inch chest of drawers (unfinished); wood-carving tools (available at hobby stores); fine sandpaper; maple stain; raw umber and crimson artists' oil paints; linseed oil; Grumbacher Tuffilm spray (available at art stores); turpentine; varnish; medium round oil brush; stain and varnish brush; wiping cloths; carbon paper; white paper.

INSTRUCTIONS:
Enlarge the patterns, *left,* onto white paper. With carbon paper and a ball-point pen, trace the patterns onto the drawer fronts; flop the patterns for the other halves of the drawer fronts. Draw the letters for the name in the space left open on the middle drawer. *Note:* You may need to adapt the design to fit a chest of a different size.

Using wood-carving tools, carve along the lines (see photo 1, *opposite*). A small curved gouge is good for single curved lines. For wider arcs, use a larger curved gouge; carve out and away to achieve the varying widths. For straight lines, use a straight chisel or V-gouge to form large grooves. *Note:* If you use inexpensive wood, take care when rounding the curves to avoid excessive chipping.

When the design is completely carved out, sand all the surfaces.

Brush maple stain on the entire chest. With a cloth, wipe away excess stain, leaving stain in the grooves (see photo 2). Let the stain dry overnight.

Paint colors onto the drawer fronts (see photo 3). Mix a small amount of crimson oil paint with linseed oil to make a light rose-colored stain. With a small paintbrush, stain the areas shown in gray on the pattern; let dry. With raw umber, paint the dark lines and areas indicated on the pattern. Let the paint dry for three days.

Spray the finished piece with Tuffilm (see photo 4) to set the paint; varnish. Clean the brushes with turpentine.

STAINED FLOOR

Another crafts project that's a guaranteed eye-catcher is the geometric-patterned stained floor shown on the opposite page. The most difficult part of the project is the initial preparation: Before you can create the pattern, you must first strip, sand, and clean the floor so that not a trace of the old finish remains. Once you've completed this chore, mark the floor with an 8-inch-square pattern, as shown *at right.* Tape 2-inch-wide masking tape inside *every* other square (see pattern).

Once the pattern is complete, stain the 8-inch squares orange, and the 4-inch squares reddish-brown. Let the stain dry overnight. When you're sure that the stain has completely dried, remove the tape and varnish the floor.

STAINED FLOOR

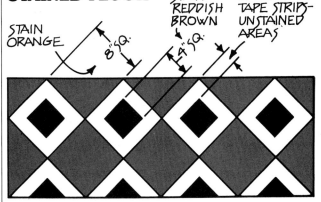

STAIN ORANGE

STAIN REDDISH BROWN

2" WIDE TAPE STRIPS— UNSTAINED AREAS

8" SQ.

4" SQ.

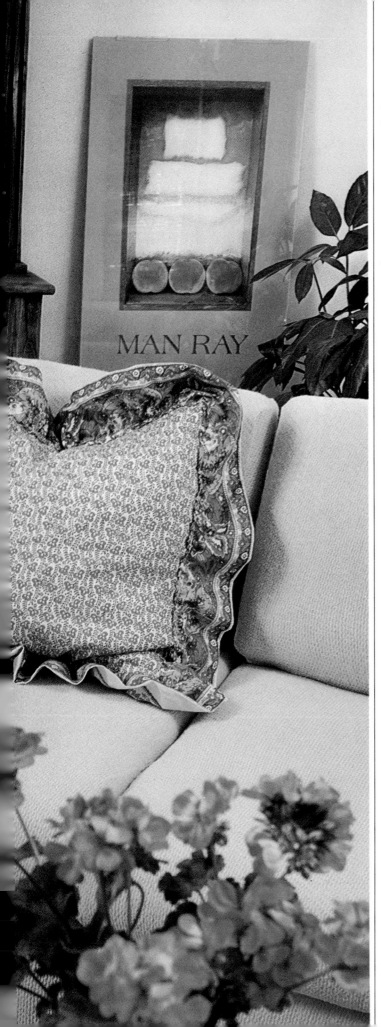

Easy Updates

Timeworn sofas and other upholstered pieces can really have a depressing effect on a room. If you have a sofa that's sad looking but structurally sound, there's no point in tossing it out. You can save the sofa (and money, too) with a ready-made slipcover like this one.

Purchased from a well-known mail-order catalog, the inexpensive stretch slipcover has been given a classy custom look with the addition of a skirted border. Since just a small amount of fabric is needed to make the gathered skirt, you might want to splurge on something really special, like this French floral pattern hand-printed on cotton. Pillows covered in a related fabric and dressed with their own matching borders tie the scheme together.

No house or apartment is immune from contracting a case of the blahs. Eventually, even the most beautiful room scheme is going to look worse for the wear. Perhaps it's the trusty old sofa that starts to look seedy, or walls and ceilings that look like they've seen better days. Whatever the problem, there's aways a cure. Here are eight pages of easy and attractive antidotes to consider.

state sales and consign-
ment shops are good places
to look for high-quality used
furniture at bargain prices.
Although the upholstery of a
used piece may look tattered
and worn, the frame—if it's in
good condition—might be
well worth saving. Once
you've determined that the
sofa or chair has redeeming
virtues, the next step is to
have the piece slipcovered or
reupholstered.

Several of the seating
pieces in this living room are
secondhand. They've been
given a fresh new look with
white muslin slipcovers. After
cutting the inexpensive muslin
sheeting to furniture size, the
homeowner quilted the pieces
with polyester fiberfill, then
had an upholsterer make the
slipcovers.

The master bath in this 60-year-old house suffered from problems inherent with age. Although the ceramic tile was still in good condition, the plaster ceiling was crumbling. The handsome, save-money design solution was to cover the ceiling with a lattice panel. Both the ceiling and the panel are painted a rich rust shade picked up from the small-print wallpaper.

The medicine cabinet trim is painted to match the ceiling. The decorative accent piece above the cabinet is a simple-to-construct "tray box" with three large scallop shells glued to the surface.

Crating lumber is the least expensive wood you can buy. Here it's been used to create a distinctive wall treatment in a tiny bathroom. The precut strips are spaced ¾ inch apart and are nailed directly to the wall. Painted a subtle gray, the wooden strips do a beautiful job of hiding the residue of old plastic tile that had been chipped from the drywall. If you decide to use crating lumber for a similar wall application, we suggest that you carefully handpick each piece to make sure the wood isn't warped.

The ceramic tile that surrounds the tub was green to begin with. Now, thanks to epoxy paint, it's white.

If there's a budding young artist or two in your family, consider creating a padded wall like this one. The no-fuss treatment allows children to pin up their masterpieces without damaging the walls. Another plus for padded walls is that they disguise cracked or irregular surfaces.

The padding technique is simple. First, fasten wide lengths of cotton or polyester batting to the wall with a staple gun. Next, cut fabric pieces slightly wider than the padding and staple them over the batting. To hide the seams, add lengths of welting or other coordinating trim.

The wall fabric shown here is heavy-duty cotton, but you could effectively use any tightly woven fabric that's not likely to stretch or show pin marks.

Four inexpensive India-print bed throws were used to beautify the walls in this kitchen breakfast nook. Purchased at a store that specializes in merchandise from the Orient, the twin-size cotton throws were cut to fit the wall area, then pasted in place.

To create this unique type of fabric wall treatment, first measure the wall area from floor to ceiling and from corner to corner to determine how many 72x108-inch bed throws you'll need. Cut off and save the borders. Starting at a corner of the room, tack one panel of cloth at the ceiling line. Have someone hold up the cloth while you apply transparent wallpaper paste directly on the wall. Pat the fabric to the wall, and work down to the floor. Repeat this step until all panels are up.

For decorative effect (and to conceal the seams and spaces between fabric panels), apply the borders you cut off earlier. To finish, spread transparent wallpaper paste or fabric protector over the fabric-covered wall.

A shirred wall treatment is an excellent solution for a room in need of a softening influence. Newer apartments and houses with stark, featureless walls are particularly good candidates for shirred fabric treatments.

Here a variety of blue-and-white batik prints was used to create a focal point and add a feeling of warmth on one wall of this small living room. Lengths of fabric are tightly gathered on curtain rods at the ceiling line, then stretched taut to get the soft, shirred effect. Sheets would work equally well.

White mini-slat blinds and a plain sisal floor covering keep the multipatterned scheme from overpowering the room.

Unfinished Finds

Unfinished furniture offers a fabulous way to stretch your decorating dollars. If you still think of "unfinished" in terms of stapled-together construction and so-so styling, you're in for some nice surprises. The make-do quality of the past has been replaced by good workmanship, handsome woods, and pleasing designs. Another advantage of today's unfinished furniture is savings. Although prices aren't in the bargain basement range, they are generally less than those of similar pre-finished items.

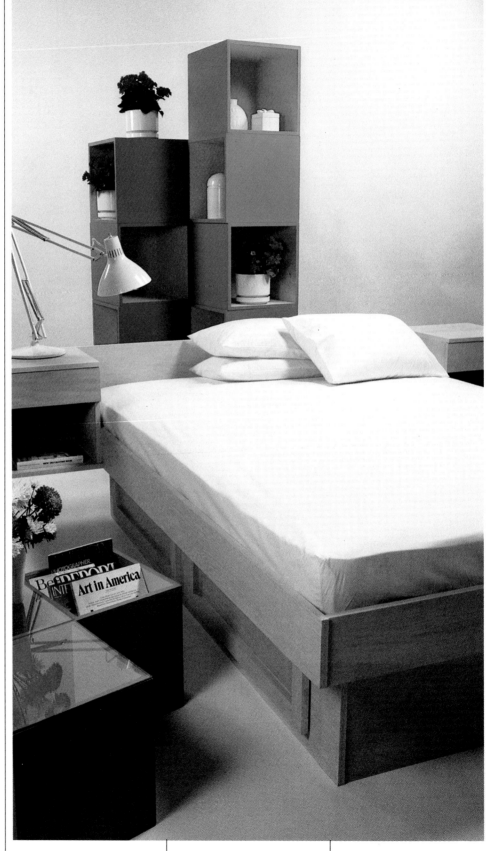

Perhaps the best advantage of unfinished furniture is flexibility. You decide on the wood tone, the color, and the finish you like. In addition, you get the personal satisfaction of creating your own "work of art."

At right are several examples of unfinished pieces with contemporary styling. The oak platform bed has been given a natural, bleached-look finish with a coat of neutral wood stain. The bed boasts a headboard with matching nightstands and storage drawers at the bottom of the cantilevered base.

The stackable storage cubes are made of particleboard. These have been painted, but you could also cover them with fabric or wallpaper. (Note: In addition to providing storage and display space, the cubes can be turned upside down and used as tables.)

At long last, it's possible to find unfinished furniture in a wide variety of styles. Whether your tastes run toward traditional, contemporary, English, French, or Early American design, you should have little trouble finding pieces to suit your preference.

At left, a French Régence armchair and a grouping of simple-lined Parsons tables are teamed for contrast. The chair's soft yellow finish is easy to achieve. First apply a coat of white oil-base enamel, then brush on an oak stain (after the enamel has dried). Then, before the stain dries, rub it off. This produces the nice milky glaze.

The Parsons tables have been snazzed up with stripes of black-and-white paint.

A corner cabinet like this one, *right,* has a built-in, custom look at a do-it-yourself price. A coat of protective paste wax is all it took to bring out the natural beauty of the knotty pine. Pumpkin orange paint provides a colorful accent for the cupboard interior and the inner sides of the paned glass doors.

The tavern chair, a classic design from the 1800s, sports an unexpectedly colorful finish, achieved with a neutral wood stain that's tinted with blue colorant.

To create a similar finish, simply brush on a coat of blue stain, wipe it off while it's still fairly wet, then (when the piece is dry) apply a coat or two of glossy polyurethane for surface protection.

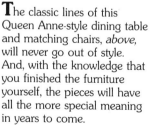

The classic lines of this Queen Anne-style dining table and matching chairs, *above*, will never go out of style. And, with the knowledge that you finished the furniture yourself, the pieces will have all the more special meaning in years to come.

In lieu of a stain, three coats of a rich Danish oil were applied to highlight the wood grain of the chairs and the herringbone design of the oak parquet tabletop.

Here are several more examples of furniture with roots in the past, *right*. The three go-anywhere nesting tables have been beautifully finished with a rich mahogany stain and a high-gloss varnish. The result is an expensive lacquer look for much less cost.

The exquisite Queen Anne-style "lady's desk" is made of elegant cherry wood. It's finished with a one-step cherry stain and sealer and covered with a mirrorlike coat of polyurethane.

You'll find these attractive butcher-block pieces, *left,* useful for the kitchen, dining room, family room, or hobby center. They're specially designed to stand up to hard daily use. Teamed with the maple table and the matching pot rack is an oak paddle-splat, bow-back chair. Butcher block furniture comes unfinished and is best left that way. An occasional application of oil will keep the wood looking good for years.

Simple designs like this pine pencil-post bed and mission-style rocking chair, *right,* call for equally simple finishes. A one-step maple-tone stain and sealer brings out the best of the pine wood and enhances the old-time look. A coat of flat polyurethane adds an extra measure of protection for the porous wood.

Shiny white enamel on the rocking chair is not only good looking, but practical, too. With this type of finish, the chair is suitable for use on a porch or in the parlor.

Here are two more examples of unfinished furniture that answer today's living needs. The compact stereo "stack" with smoked-glass doors holds all kinds of electronic gear in a sliver of vertical space. The oak piece is finished with paint, stain, and polyurethane.

The modular pine storage system comes K-D (knocked down); you put it together yourself. The system includes optional doors, shelves, and drawers, and is amenable to a variety of finishes. This system sports a pleasing combination of yellow, orange, and black paint.

Here's more proof that unfinished furniture comes in all sizes, shapes, and styles. The three pieces shown *above*, though disparate in origin, are compatible in appearance and use.

The pine rolltop desk comes in a box for quick assembly. It's been finished with a maple stain-sealer and topped with a satin varnish.

The five-shelf étagère sports a snazzy neutral wood stain that's been laced with a green colorant. This kind of finishing technique lets you add color to an unfinished piece without covering up the wood grain.

Flat black paint adds dash to the inexpensive rush-seat ladder-back chair. But black isn't your only choice. With unfinished furniture, you can finish your project with any color imaginable.

Up-to-the-minute designs like these, *above,* can solve the space-squeeze problem in a child's room. The sturdy pine system includes the clean-lined bunk beds, the youth-size desk, and (not shown here) a chair and a matching shelf unit.

The furniture is wonderfully flexible. All of the pieces can be separated, arranged, and rearranged to suit changing space and living requirements. As the children get older, the beds can be "de-bunked" for a more grown-up look in a teenager's room. (Remember, you'll save money over the years by buying furniture that will "grow" with your child.)

Two coats of flat varnish provide the unfinished pieces with an extra-durable finish that won't wear easily. Colorful paint offers yet another attractive finish possibility.

Budget-priced particleboard furniture takes well to decorative, do-it-yourself projects. The bookcase and child-size wardrobe pictured *above* were brightened up with paint and wallpaper border appliqués. The wardrobe has hanging space on one side and four drawers on the other; the height is just right for a small child.

A Parsons-style end table makes a perfect worktable for a youngster. This one was painted fire-engine red. Two wooden cubes become durable stools with storage space inside. The white cubes were stippled with black paint for decorative effect. This same stipple treatment was used on the top of the wardrobe.

Save with Sheets and Fabric

chapter

11

On-sale bed sheets are still one of the best bargains around. If you are the slightest bit handy with a needle and thread, you can use versatile sheets for all kinds of decorating projects. They offer a lot of yardage for the money and are available in a vast selection of pretty colors, patterns, and prints. Fabric remnants are another good bargain.

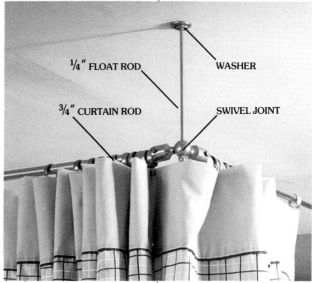

¼" FLOAT ROD   WASHER
¾" CURTAIN ROD   SWIVEL JOINT

Even non-sewers can create a fabric four-poster like this one, *left*. The tailored treatment consists of four top sheets hung on brass café curtain rings. Unless you need to hem the sheets, the treatment is a no-sew project.

The wraparound rail is made of adjustable brass curtain rods, connected by brass swivel joints. (Look for them at a drapery hardware store and specify joints with ¼-inch holes through the center.) The verticals are pieces of brass plumbing float rod, threaded three inches at both ends. A plumbing supply house will cut and thread them on the spot.

To assemble, first drill holes in the ceiling for toggle bolts. Screw ¼-inch toggles to float rods and insert into ceiling holes. Secure rods with washers and nuts.

Attach swivel joints to the rods and cap the ends with brass cap nuts. Now, screw brass sockets (another drapery hardware item) to the wall. Once the framework is complete, hang sheets or other fabric with handy clip-on curtain rings.

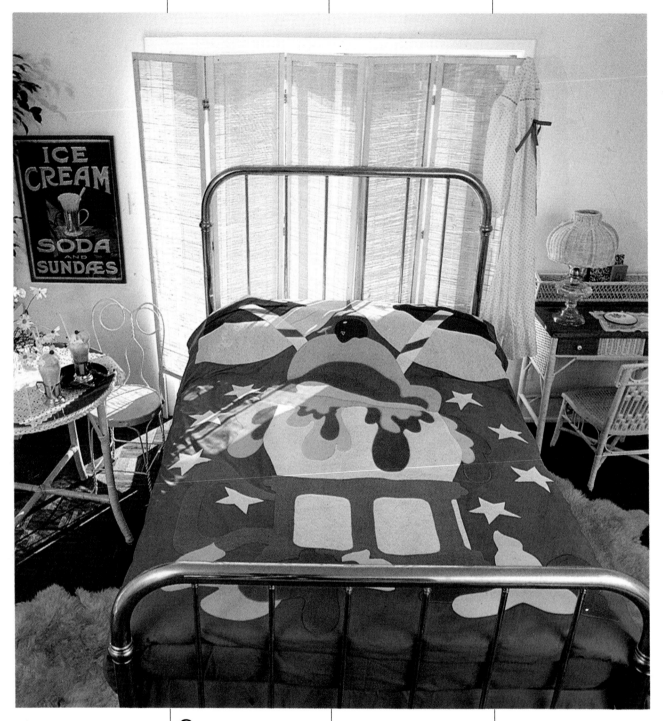

Comforter covers, also known as "duvets," not only protect a comforter from dust and dirt, but offer a nice decorative touch. Either buy ready-made comforter covers or create a custom look (and save money, too) by making your own.

This ice cream soda comforter cover is made from bed sheets and felt appliqué. The comforter itself is made of down and comes from a kit that you sew and stuff by yourself. (More money can be saved by using synthetic filling in lieu of down.)

The lightweight felt is a special kind that makes appliqué work a breeze. No sewing or turning under edges is required; you simply iron the felt cutouts onto the sheet (the iron melts the glue on the back of the felt and bonds it to the fabric). In no time, you have a down coverlet to keep you warm and a piece of art to cover your bed.

With a little help from you, a mundane mover's blanket can be transformed into a magnificent Amish-style quilt like this one, *above*. Mover's blankets are available at most art supply stores in a variety of sizes and colors. Besides being durable and thrifty, they're prequilted—a big timesaving bonus.

This quilt is made from eight prequilted fabric diamonds pieced to form an eight-pointed star. The star is appliquéd, then bordered by pieced fabric strips. To make the star motif, you will need 1½ yards each of 45-inch-wide deep red and light red prequilted fabric. You'll also need ½ yard each of red and purple prequilted fabric.

For the diamond pattern, cut a 14x30-inch paper rectangle. Fold the rectangle in half crosswise and in half again lengthwise, then unfold. Draw lines from the ends of the vertical folded lines to the ends of the horizontal lines, forming a diamond. Using this diamond pattern, cut four diamonds each of deep red and light red prequilted fabric. Cut the remaining fabric in 5½-inch-wide strips. (This includes the half-yard pieces of red and purple fabric.)

To make the star, piece the diamonds together along two sides, interchanging colors as you stitch (refer to the photo). Use ½-inch seam allowances and carefully position the points at the star center. Press the seams open and the remaining seams under ½ inch. Hand-sew the star to the quilt center.

Patch the strips together end-to-end in random lengths. Press the raw edges of the strip under ½ inch. Cut the strip into four sections to fit around the star; pin strips in place. Cut away the excess fabric and machine-stitch the sections in place.

No matter how small your budget, there's no reason to settle for a dull, nondescript decorating scheme. This bedroom, *left,* was spruced up for next to nothing—simply by making use of on-sale, discontinued sheets. Several sets of pretty, floral-pattern bed linens were used to make pillow shams, a dust ruffle, a tie-on chair cushion, and sprightly pouf shades for the windows. Dusty pink wall paint unifies the setting and adds an extra measure of decorative impact.

Here's another example of how to use sheets to spruce up a room. In this instance, *above,* sheets do more than make a strong decorative statement; they solve a furniture placement problem as well. Because the room is quite small, the only place to put the bed is in front of a large expanse of glass. By using a single sheet pattern at the window and on the bed, what could have been an awkward arrangement is now a unified whole.

By incorporating the window into the decorating scheme, the room looks larg-er and less chopped up. The treatment includes a ruffled valance, a fabric-laminated roller shade, and tieback draperies. The lavish use of sheet fabric extends to the upholstered headboard, a pair of lamp shades, the table skirt, and a new seat cushion for the old wicker chair.

To dress up a decor with art nouveau elegance, try your hand at this lavish-looking felt appliqué room divider. The results are quite eye-catching, and the technique couldn't be easier. Just cut flourishes and florals from brightly colored felt, then glue the pieces onto panels of fabric. Staple each panel to a wooden frame, then add hinges. No sewing is required to complete the three-panel screen.

The same type of felt design can quickly be translated into other easy-to-accomplish projects. For instance, use a similar large-scale floral pattern to create a wall hanging or a window covering. Small motifs will enhance a photo album cover or a tote bag. Or, for a fast fix-up, apply them to children's clothing.

Here are two more ways to use inexpensive fabric for practical and decorative purposes. In the room *at left*, an old table gets a new lease on life with a felt-and-appliqué cover-up. The embellishments are flower motifs cut from a sheet and glued to a large piece of brown felt.

The softly shirred wall treatment is elegant and easy to effect. Simply stitch wide pockets into the tops and bottoms of sheets that have been cut to the desired length, then gather the fabric onto two-inch-wide strips of wood. Use small finishing nails to tack the fabric and wood slats to the wall.

Has your dining room furniture seen better days? Before you give your chairs the old heave-ho, consider this very simple—and stylish—solution. A quick sew-up sack hides the dinette-set look of these chrome-and-cane chairs. The cloth covers are sewn inside-out (so the seams won't show), then slipped over the chairs. The covers can easily be removed for cleaning simply by placing a zipper at the foot of each sack.

The two old café tables have been similarly updated with new black laminate tops and a coat of black paint on the pedestal bases.

chapter

12

Dollarwise Windows

There are numerous ways you can fashion a handsome window treatment without spending a fortune. Just remember: the less elaborate the treatment, the more money you're bound to save.

Simple window solutions not only save money, they're generally the best looking, too. *Above,* mock balloon shades add softness to these large-paned windows without impairing the view.

To make a similar treatment, begin with a lined panel of fabric that measures twice the width and about half the length of the window. Sew rod casings at the top, bottom, and center of the panel. Shirr the fabric onto three curtain rods, then mount so that the fullness between the rods creates the ballooned effect.

This minimal window treatment, *right,* preserves the view and offers privacy at the same time. In addition, the treatment is a practical solution for a series of windows that individually open inward.

To make the panels, buy enough fabric to measure twice the width of the window being covered. First, fold over several inches of fabric at the top and bottom of each panel, then seam the folds to form pockets at each end. Slip brass rods through the pockets; install four brass brackets on the window and secure the rods in place.

Here, simple ties are made of the same red-and-white polka-dot material used for the fabric panels.

Traditionally, a swag is a formal treatment used to top draperies—a look that requires yards and yards of fabric and an experienced hand to create. But this simple-to-make swag, *left,* can solo beautifully without the usual companion draperies. The treatment adds a nice touch of class to this unpretentious double-hung window.

The lightweight calico fabric is interfaced to help it maintain its graceful shape. If you use heavier fabric, the interfacing can be omitted. Here, a rosy pink-colored lining backs the gentle folds of the side-hanging calico jabots.

The center festoon and two side jabots are stapled to a wooden valance placed just above the window frame. Calico rosettes are affixed to each corner to conceal the adjoining pleats. A roll-up shade installed behind the swag offers privacy when needed, but doesn't detract from the treatment.

Not all windows require or need a decorative treatment. Some—particularly those that lack a decent view—can be camouflaged completely, or put to practical use. If you have a small room with very little wall space, then by all means consider putting your window to "work."

The window pictured *above* is located in a hobby workshop. Rather than let the glass area go to waste, the entire window has been turned into a shelved storage area. The utilitarian treatment consists of sturdy planking supported by metal shelf standards and brackets. The shelves can be adjusted up or down to hold and display all sizes of crafts and hobby paraphernalia. With this kind of treatment, there's little loss of natural light, but a big gain in storage space.

A great way to dramatize standard windows is to frame them with fabric-covered lambrequins. And, if you go one step further and paint your walls with high-gloss paint in a contrasting color, you're guaranteed a knockout combination.

This bedroom, *left*, features 12-inch-wide plywood lambrequins that are covered with black canvas fabric. You can create a similar upholstered look by stretching fabric over quilt batting, then stapling the fabric to the back side of a plywood frame.

White mini-slat blinds complete this simple, but sophisticated, treatment.

A plain white roller shade is one of the least costly window treatments available. But you needn't settle for plainness. For a few extra dollars you can fashion a stylish, custom-looking shade like the one pictured *above*.

Start with a standard, inexpensive shade, then jazz it up with vinylized wallpaper or fabric. You can glue, staple, or laminate a covering to just about any shade. Laminating kits (available at paint and wallpaper stores) make short work of the project. They come with everything you need, including the shade cloth and the roller. If you decide to use glue, be sure to use non-staining, diluted white glue for best results.

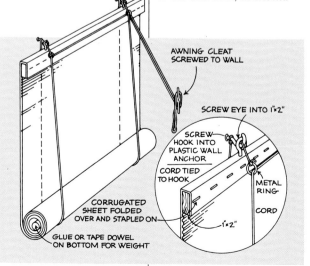

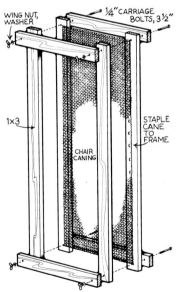

WING NUT, WASHER

¼" CARRIAGE BOLTS, 3½"

1×3

CHAIR CANING

STAPLE CANE TO FRAME

This make-it-yourself window treatment, *above,* features ready-made sheet caning that's sandwiched between strips of clear pine. The caning, which comes in widths from 14 to 21 inches, can be left natural or painted.

To make this treatment, first cut 1x3s and lay out boards to form a double frame. Drill holes through each corner. Next, insert carriage bolts through holes in the top of the frame, then staple the caning to the reverse side. Lastly, overlap long boards with short crosspieces. Cap the bolts with washers and wing nuts, then hinge the frame to the window. The illustration *at left* will help you get the picture.

Corrugated cardboard (the kind used as a packing material) can be used to create a nifty roll-up shade like this one, *above.* The inexpensive cardboard comes in 6-foot-wide rolls, and is quite sturdy.

Making the shade is a snap. Begin by cutting a strip of cardboard at least two feet longer than the length of the window to be covered. Staple the cut piece to a length of 1x2 wood strip, as shown in the diagram, *below,* and

screw in a couple of screw eyes. Hold the shade in place against the window to see where to put the screw hooks in the wall.

When you string up the cord, start with two lengths at least four times as long as the blind itself (cut off any excess later). Tie the cords to each screw hook behind the shade; run the cord down, underneath, and up the front, through the metal rings tied to the screw hooks, and over to the wall cleat, as shown.

AWNING CLEAT SCREWED TO WALL

SCREW EYE INTO 1×2"

SCREW HOOK INTO PLASTIC WALL ANCHOR

CORD TIED TO HOOK

METAL RING

CORD

1×2"

CORRUGATED SHEET FOLDED OVER AND STAPLED ON

GLUE OR TAPE DOWEL ON BOTTOM FOR WEIGHT

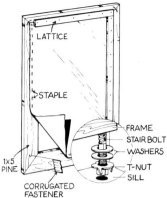

LATTICE

STAPLE

1x5
PINE

CORRUGATED
FASTENER

FRAME
STAIR BOLT
WASHERS
T-NUT
SILL

Here's a great way to cover up an ugly window (or an unsightly view) without totally blocking the light. Looking somewhat like a Japanese shoji screen, the window panel is made of pine and (of all things) mosquito netting. The panel swivels on a pivot system, allowing easy access to the window behind.

The frame consists of pine 1x5s that are mitered, glued, then connected with ½-inch No. 5 corrugated fasteners. Mosquito netting is stapled to the frame's back; strips of lattice cover the staples. The frame itself is attached to the windowsill, top and bottom, with ¼-inch stair bolts. Each bolt looks like a screw with two threaded ends. The tapered end goes into the frame; the straight end fits into the sill.

To ensure that the frame swings freely, the bolts are screwed into T-nuts that are a *size larger* (5/16 inch) than the bolt. Washers separate the frame and the sill to keep things working smoothly.

The installation is similar to putting in a sliding door: the hole that the bolt slips into at the top is deeper than the bottom hole. The frame slips into the top hole first, leaving room for the bottom to clear the sill.

SHADES

Gone are the days when white was the only choice in window shades, and crocheted pulls were *de rigueur*. Today's shades are so stylish that they can be used in place of curtains and draperies. They're available in decorator colors, coordinating patterns, and clothlike textures. Shown here is but a small sampling of current shade styles.

Some shades even help you save money by cutting down on energy costs. The white mesh shade, *near right*, keeps interiors cool by cutting out the sun's hottest rays. The pleated shade, *far right*, features an aluminum backing that reflects 60 percent of the summer sun and heat. During the winter months, the process is reversed—49 percent of the heated air is reflected back into the room. Custom-fit shades also are available.

WOVEN WOODS

Woven wood shades are hard to beat when you're looking for a decorative and energy-efficient window treatment. Wood is an excellent natural insulator, and when teamed with thick, tightly woven yarn, it provides good protection against heat loss.

A wide variety of woven wood styles is on the market today. You can choose a design that is predominantly wood, or a heavily woven shade that has only a hint of wood showing. The slats themselves range from light to dark wood tones.

Although all of the woven wood shades pictured here feature natural-hued yarns, brightly colored versions also are available.

There's usually more than one way to treat any given window; the problem is knowing what your various options are. With so many sizes and shapes to contend with, it's easy to get confused. To help you make the best choice, here are six pages of treatment solutions for the most common window shapes.

SINGLE WINDOWS

Double-hung sash windows are by far the most common type. Although they're receptive to a variety of treatments, they tend to look skimpy if placed singly on a wall.

1. Make a small window look larger than it is with two tiers of café curtains. For best results, the rods should be wider than the window itself, and the lower curtain should extend to the floor.

2. Give decorative importance to a standard window by combining floor-length, tie-back curtains with a shirred fabric wall treatment.

3. Add instant drama to a double-hung window with floor-to-ceiling foldbacks. Hang the two flat panels from double curtain rods, one in front of the other. When folded back, the underpanel becomes a design element.

4. Build a wooden lambrequin (frame) around a window to make it appear taller than it is. Paint or upholster the frame with fabric, then team with vertical blinds.

5. Team floor-length traverse draperies with mini-slat blinds to create a softened, elongated look.

6. Hide a window air conditioner with a decorative four-panel screen. Cover the rest of the window with pleated draperies that fall just below the top of the screen.

7. Camouflage an ugly window with a combination of shutters and drapery panels. The top two tiers of shutters open for ventilation. The lower tier is stationary.

WINDOW SKETCHBOOK

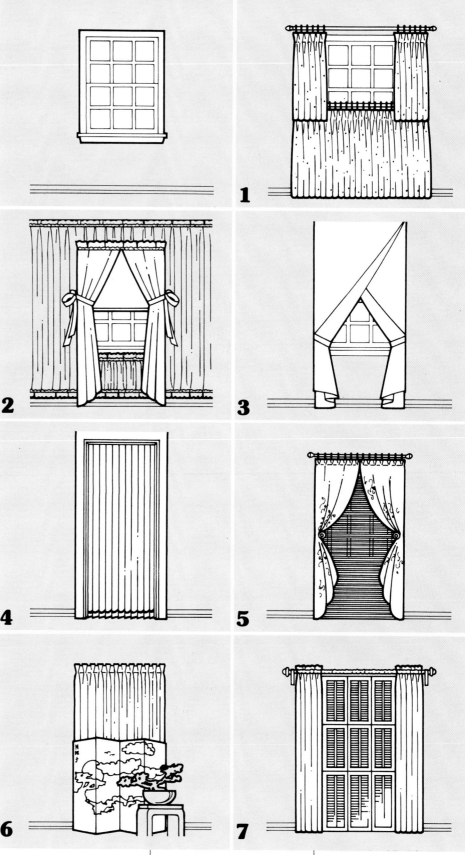

CORNER WINDOWS

Of all the tricky window situations, corner windows pose the greatest problems. Their edge-to-edge placement makes for awkward hardware installation, thereby limiting the number of treatment options. A corner placement also makes furniture arrangement somewhat difficult. There *are* attractive solutions, however. Here are seven to consider:

1. A simple solution is to hang two panels of floor-length draperies from individual one-way traverse rods or café rods and rings. If you wish, add roll-up matchstick blinds—mounted on the window casings—for a textured, light-filtering accent.

2. This double-shirred corner window treatment is a fashionable twist on an old favorite—curtains and sheers. Above each window are two sets of double curtain rods; one double rod is positioned over the casing and the second is mounted on the wall eight to ten inches above. Sheers are hung on the inside rods; tiebacks are placed on the outside.

3. Position floor-to-ceiling bifold screens beside each of the windows for a trim, contemporary look. At the ceiling line, hang window-length Roman shades. Use the same fabric to cover the screens, or use a different fabric in a harmonizing color.

4. Swags teamed with shutters are a good choice for corner windows—especially in a colonial setting. Fill in the area beneath the windows with leafy plants or a skirted table topped with accessories.

5. Make a window look larger with floor-to-ceiling draperies and mini-slat blinds. A corner-turning valance will tie the treatment together.

6. Try woven woods as draperies, with slats running vertically instead of horizontally. Use heavy-duty rods to support the weight.

7. Similar in style to treatment number 5, this option uses inexpensive bamboo shades in lieu of blinds.

WINDOW SKETCHBOOK

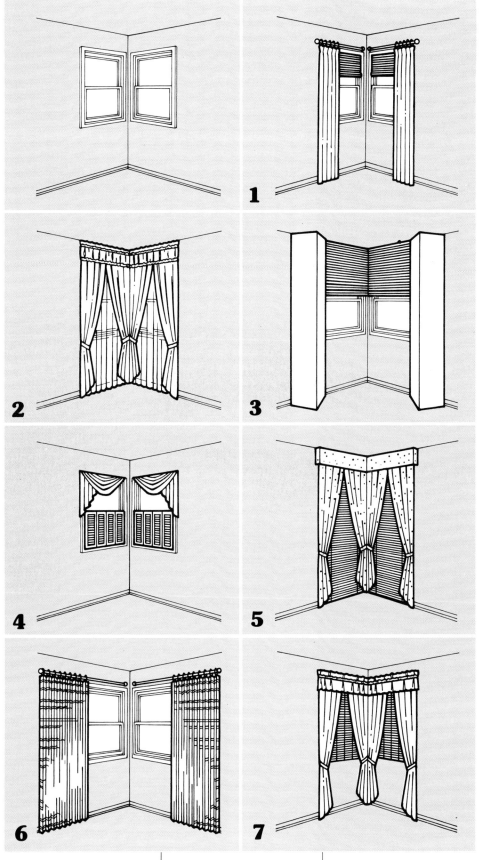

IN-SWINGING CASEMENTS

Casement windows come in several varieties—those that crank outward toward the exterior of the house and those that swing inward. The former can be treated like ordinary sash windows, but the latter requires a treatment that won't interfere with the window when it's opened.

1. Here, a curtain rod is mounted on each window, allowing one or both windows to open individually. Simple sash curtains, also on separate rods, cover the lower half of each window.

2. Textured woven woods fashioned into Roman shades make a terrific treatment for casement windows. When mounted at the ceiling line, the shade can be fully raised, allowing full access to the windows.

3. Traverse draperies can be used when the rod is mounted above the window opening. Make sure the rod is longer than the window itself so that the draperies, when opened, stack neatly to the side of the windows.

4. A more formal version of the traverse treatment makes use of an inside rod for operable sheers and a fabric-covered cornice as well. Be sure to situate the cornice and all hardware well above the window.

5. Individual sash curtains, gathered cottage style with a ribbon or fabric tie, are an easy and economical solution for in-swinging windows.

6. Four sliding fabric panels, hung from a special track system mounted at the ceiling line, create a clean-lined contemporary treatment. Two of the floor-to-ceiling panels slide to the left; the others slide to the right.

7. Swinging crane rods, one above each window, open into the room like the windows themselves. Choose lightweight fabric for best results; tie back the curtains or let them hang loosely.

WINDOW SKETCHBOOK

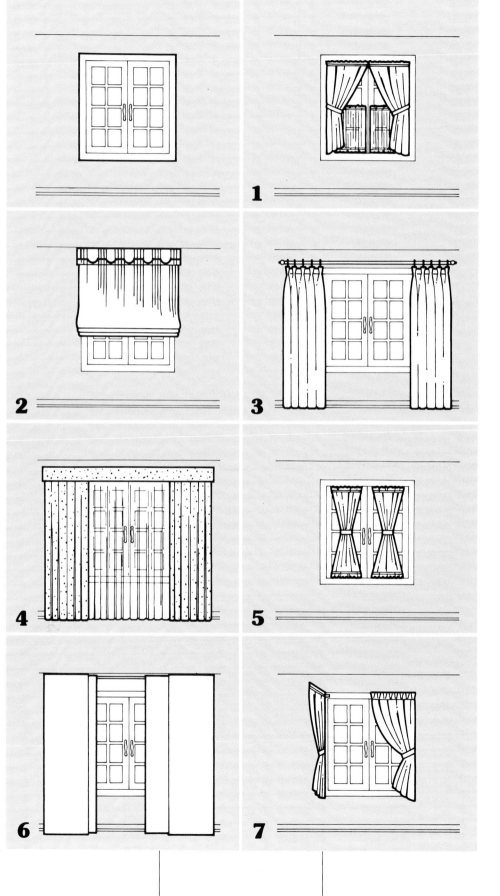

WINDOW SKETCHBOOK

TWO- OR THREE-WINDOW SERIES

A series of windows makes a handsome focal point in any room. You can cover each window individually or treat the series as a single unit. In either case, strive for a unified effect.

1. Floor-length tiebacks hung from one heavy-duty rod are teamed here with individual roller shades for privacy and energy control. Choose among light-filtering shades, fabric-laminated shades, or any number of custom variations.

2. Balloon shades made from lightweight, translucent fabric or from a polished cotton print offer a high-fashion look. Use one large shade for all three windows or three separate shades and an overall valance.

3. Mini-slat blinds provide understated styling plus effective light and privacy control. Use the mini-slats alone or add side draperies for a softer touch. For a more rustic or country look, use wooden mini-slats instead of metal.

4. A lambrequin is simply an enlarged cornice that extends down the sides of a window. In this example, a triple lambrequin (made of plywood) is effectively used to provide sharp definition for a series of windows. The top portion of the lambrequin covers the hardware of the three woven wood blinds and is deep enough to handle the bulk of the blind material when the shades are raised.

5. Here a single Roman shade provides streamlined unity for a triple window.

6. Bottoms-up shades can be mounted at floor level to disguise a window's dimensions, making a high-placed window look elongated. Draperies used in conjunction with shades will exaggerate the window width.

7. This triple window is decoratively framed with fabric-covered bifold screens and privacy-lending shirred curtains at the lower third of the window.

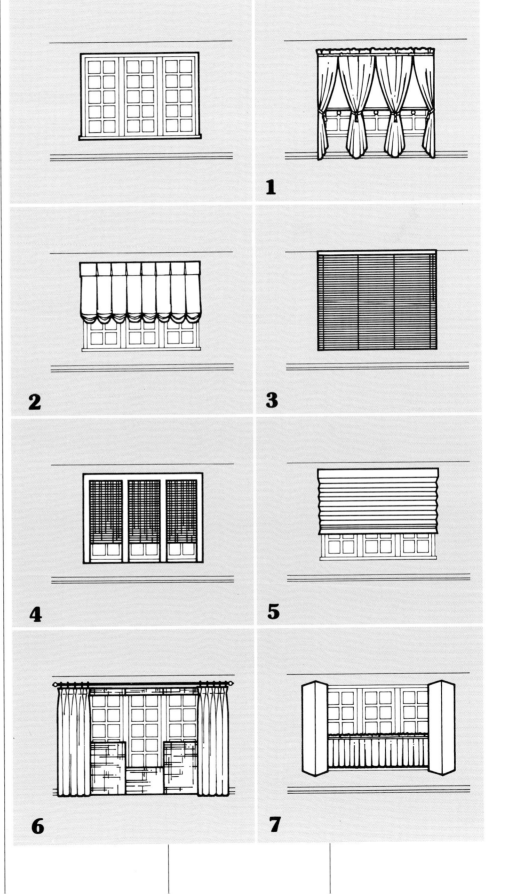

SLIDING GLASS DOORS

Sliding glass doors are the contemporary counterpart of traditional French doors. As popular as they are in today's homes, their stark design and large proportions can make them difficult to ease gracefully into a room scheme. The problem, of course, is devising a treatment that won't interfere with the proper functioning of the sliding doors.

1. Fabric panels that slide from one side to the other on a special track create a tailored treatment for sliding doors. Use three or four panels to cover the doors. If space permits, install a track that's wider than the double doors so the panels can stack beside the doors.

2. Two roller shades mounted on the wall above the doors offer another solution for sliding doors. Hide the rollers and hardware with a painted or fabric-covered lambrequin.

3. Folding screens placed on either side of a sliding glass door provide a perfect "hiding place" for traverse draperies when they're drawn back. For a unified effect, cover the screens with fabric or paint to match the walls.

4. A pair of woven wood blinds can be used to effectively cover sliding glass doors. Mount the blinds on the wall above the doors and, if you wish, unite the pair of blinds with a valance.

5. Custom-made latticework panels that hang from and slide along an overhead track (like closet doors) disguise the track and visually unite the lattice panels.

6. Vertical-louvered blinds are ideal for sliding doors. Not only do they turn 180 degrees to allow light to enter the room, but they also slide to one side of the doors.

7. Floor-to-ceiling louvered shutters provide another possibility for sliding doors. The louvers can be opened to let in light, or the shutters themselves can be folded back to allow access to the door.

WINDOW SKETCHBOOK

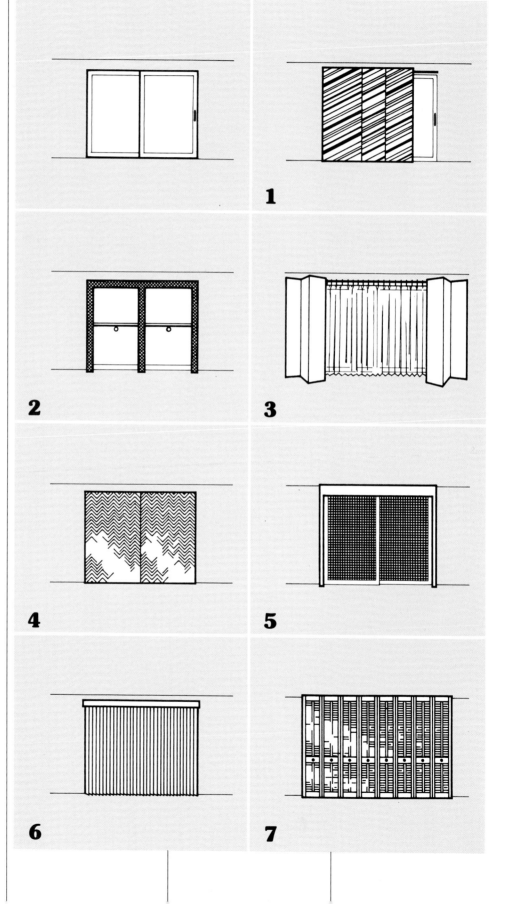

BAY WINDOWS

Bay windows are coveted for the beauty they lend to a room, but they're not the easiest of windows to decorate. Bays can be a combination of sash windows, picture windows, casements, or louvered windows, so it's important to choose a treatment that is compatible with the window styling. Special traverse and curtain rods can be customized to fit the angle and measurements of any bay area.

1. A trio of woven wood blinds offers an attractive and practical treatment for a bay window area. By mounting each blind individually within the window frame, lighting needs are easily controlled.

2. These floor-to-ceiling tieback curtains are hung on stationary side-mounted crane rods. The sheers are hung on an angled rod that traverses all three windows. With this type of rod, the sheers can be fully or partially closed for sun control and privacy.

3. This treatment is a good one for bays that must accommodate a sofa or other furniture items. The side curtains are stationary, but the sill-length sheers can be drawn open without getting tangled with the furniture.

4. Floor-to-ceiling tieback draperies on each window create a pleasing traditional look. For an even more formal effect, add a sculptured valance like this one.

5. Simple ruffled curtains are a good choice for a country setting. Depending on privacy needs, use semisheer curtains with or without roll-up shades.

6. Make a small bay area look larger with a horizontal curtain treatment like this one. Use three separate rods or one custom-angled rod mounted halfway between the top edge of the window and the floor.

7. Mini-slat blinds are excellent for controlling light and privacy in a bay window area. These window-length blinds are framed with decorative wooden lambrequins.

WINDOW SKETCHBOOK

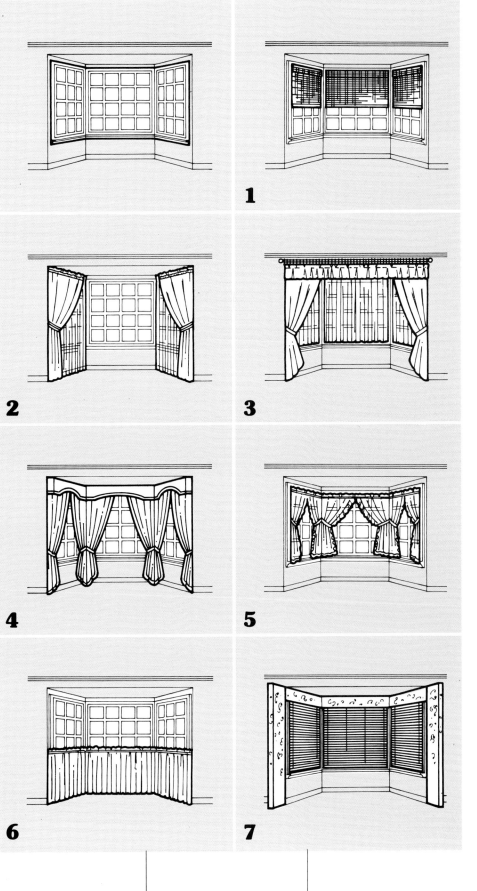

1

2

3

4

5

6

7

ENERGY-SAVING SUGGESTIONS

Do you know that as much as 30 percent of your home's total heat loss escapes through the windows? With ever-increasing utility costs, that's more than reason enough to consider using energy-saving window treatments. Here are some suggestions to help cut heating bills in winter and air-conditioning costs during hot-weather months.

The first line of defense against heat loss in winter and heat gain in summer is to trap "dead" air between the outdoors and the room itself. Storm windows or "sandwiches" of glass, with all cracks tightly weather-stripped, are essential in northern climates. Fabric is an excellent insulator, and can cut winter heat loss through glass up to 80 to 90 percent. *Any* type of fabric window treatment is better than nothing, but some are more effective than others.

DRAPERIES AND LININGS

Draperies are tops for guarding against heat loss, *if* you make a wise choice of materials and treatment styles. The more tightly woven and heavier the fabric, the better.

Custom-made draperies offer the most variety in energy-saving treatments. Most department stores will custom-make draperies with weather-resistant linings, as will stores specializing in solar materials. They usually have the lining material for sale by the yard, so you can attach a lining to existing draperies.

Some of the same aluminized fabrics used for window shades can be attached easily to draperies at the top and bottom with staples or tape. Or they may be used separately as free-hanging curtains and hung on the same hooks.

For seasonal efficiency, you may prefer a highly reflective aluminized material

laminated to vinyl and left free-hanging. It can be switched to face the window in summer and the room in winter to take advantage of its reflective properties.

One of the best insulating fabrics for drapery linings is Milium, a metallic-backed cotton cloth that has been used for years as a lining for winter coats. Milium is a fairly expensive material for a drapery lining, and often is used with high-priced, luxurious face fabrics.

Foylon, a foil-backed polyester developed from the same technology that produced silvery astronauts' space suits, is another good insulating and reflective fabric to consider.

In addition to aluminized materials, there are linings of thin or heavy cotton and of Dacron backed with foam and vinyl. These linings rely on white or silvery colors for reflection.

Vinyl backings, formerly stiff and undrapable, have lost their rubbery surface and now feature soft embossed textures that allow curtains to hang gracefully. Some vinyl backings feel like suede or soft cotton. (If the vinyl you choose is very lightweight or inexpensive, it may have a tendency to curl up at the bottom edge.)

An added benefit of many foam and vinyl linings is their room-darkening and sound-deadening qualities.

When shopping for window coverings with energy-efficient linings, be sure to check washability of the finished draperies. Some types of insulating linings can be machine washed, but others must be dry cleaned.

Ready-mades also offer curtains and draperies with insulating linings; they are available everywhere from discount stores to the most expensive home furnishings departments.

Ready-mades, of course, are considerably less expensive than custom-made draperies. As a rule, the linings will not be of the same high-quality fabrics, but many of them will be effective weather barriers.

Most ready-made linings are of cotton or Dacron, laminated to foam and vinyl, and often laminated to the drapery fabric itself. The least expensive ready-mades may have a too-thin cotton lining or thin foam backing that may deteriorate or crumble in a short time.

SHADES

Ordinary window shades also can cut heating and cooling costs. A window with a light-colored opaque roller shade, mounted within the frame, admits 47 to 54 percent less heat in summer than an un-shaded window. Even translucent shades reduce heat loss, although not to the same extent as the opaque variety.

Some regular roller shades have special sun-filtering or aluminized backings that add even more to their energy-saving abilities.

Even in winter, a window shade can help reduce heat loss. Placed on a north- or west-facing window, shades can save as much as 31 percent loss.

Specially designed energy-savers offer even more spectacular protection from cold and heat.

To reduce energy bills, look for reflective solar shades. Though made in different ways and of a variety of materials, these shades all work on the same principle: They trap dead air and bounce heat away from the room in summer or back into the room in winter.

Some solar shades look like big sheets of transparent film. When they are drawn, you can see out, but outsiders can't see in. This filmlike material is made of a reflective aluminum layer that's sandwiched between two sheets of polyester film.

These shades are not inexpensive, however. Price for a high-quality shade to fit an average-size window (6x4-foot) is $60 or more. But the investment may be worth it when you can keep out as much as 80 percent of the heat. Solar shades also control glare and filter ultraviolet rays that fade upholstery and other fabrics.

Check the thickness of the film when shopping for this type of shade. Some are made of film that is only one mil thick; three or four mils of thickness are a must for a top-quality, durable shade.

If shades made of solar film are used on extra-large windows (more than 120 inches wide), you will need a cord and reel for raising and lowering the shade.

Other reflective shades are also available. Some resemble aluminum foil, with a plain or textured surface. Others are made from quilted aluminum, with a reflective plastic film vapor barrier and a translucent fiberfill insulation. One type of shade has metallized material laminated to white vinyl, with a layer of fiber glass sandwiched between for durability. In the summer

months, you turn the silvery side toward the glass and it reflects the heat back outside. During the winter, switch the shiny surface to the room side and it will reradiate the furnace heat into the room.

Another good form of window protection is a Thermos-style shade. It actually works on the principle of a vacuum bottle. The material is made of hundreds of tiny particles, with air space sealed into each segment. The shade has a highly reflective white pigment embedded into the materials.

Still another aluminized foil shade is made of tissue-thin layers that inflate when the shade is pulled down, creating 2½ inches of dead air space in front of the window.

Solar shade material may be attached to special roller shades, with a heavy bar at the bottom to keep it from curling when drawn. Some types of foil material can be laminated to the back of regular window shades or to other fabrics.

Most of the special solar control shades must be custom-manufactured, and you may have difficulty finding all the various types in your area. Look in the Yellow Pages of the telephone directory under "Windows—Insulating Fabrics" or "Solar Equipment and Materials."

WOODEN SHADES AND BLINDS

Woven wood shades and draperies are ideal for keeping out the cold. Wood is an excellent natural insulator, and when combined with thick, tightly woven yarn, it provides very good protection against heat loss.

When shopping, make sure the slats and reeds are of

wood. Some lower-priced woven shades have slats of plastic, which do not provide as much insulation.

Woven-woods are not cheap. The more yarn used, the higher the cost, and the better the quality. Look at the back of the woven wood shade to check its energy-saving features. Hold the shade up to the light. If there is much light leakage, this represents energy leakage as well.

Although woven woods are exellent for saving energy in winter, dark woods and yarns absorb sunrays in summer, adding unwanted heat to the house. Either choose shades of light-colored woods and yarns or add a reflective roller shade to save on air-conditioning costs.

Slatted wood blinds will help keep heat in during winter, and white metal or aluminum slatted blinds will reflect summer heat. However, when used alone, slatted blinds, whether hung vertically or horizontally, do not rate as high in year-round energy savings as do most other window treatments. For one thing, blinds do not provide a close enough seal to hold the dead air between the window and room.

Wooden louvered shutters also help to some extent in retaining heat in a room, but here again, there are air leaks.

PERMANENT WEATHER SHIELDS

In addition to draperies, shades, and blinds, there also are films that coat the window glass itself, deflecting the sun's rays, and reflecting as much as 81 percent of the sun's heat. Some films have flow-on coatings of tinted liquid plastics that harden on windowpanes. Another type is

a thin sheet of plastic that bonds to the window with an adhesive or with static pressure. In some cases, aluminum particles or coatings are applied to the plastic sheets.

Other outside devices for windows include solar fiberglass screening, thermal shutters, and reflective or solar glass panels. For information about these products, check with your local lumberyard, building supply dealer, or firms specializing in solar materials and equipment.

CONSERVATION TIPS

What you do with the window treatments you use can help the energy picture, too.
• Mount blinds and draperies outside the window frames if possible. Air may leak along the edges on an inside-the-frame mounting.
• Mount draperies from floor to ceiling and be sure draperies overlap where they meet in the center. Hold the fabric firmly to the wall at each side with strips of Velcro fastener attached to the walls and sewn to the edges of the draperies. Use cornices and lambrequins to help seal tops of windows.
• In winter, always be sure to draw shades and draperies at night or on dark, overcast days. Keep them open on sunny days.
• Keep your windows clean —especially during winter months—because clean glass lets in more sun and warmth.
• Remove screens in the winter. The mesh will reduce the sun's rays by 20 percent.
• Don't just close windows. Latch them to make as tight a seal as possible.

Lighting for Less

Both decorative and functional lighting play important roles in every decorating scheme. But lighting, like everything else, can be expensive. One way to please your bank account and at the same time brighten a room is to make your own light fixtures and lamps. The lighting projects in this chapter are as easy on the budget as they are to make.

This bathroom, *right,* is illuminated with a homemade light tube that is similar in style to the high-priced, store-bought kind.

The sophisticated fixture is made from an aluminum irrigation pipe that's been painted with coral-red auto lacquer and fitted with four 250-watt halogen bulbs that screw into standard sockets. Halogen bulbs were chosen because they last longer and produce more light for their size than standard incandescent light bulbs. The tube plugs into an ordinary wall socket with a curly, contemporary cord.

This tiny, nondescript dining area was given some flair by framing one wall with small dressing room lights. You needn't be an electrician or a do-it-yourself wizard to create a similar theatrical lighting effect. The frame consists of nothing more than a simple electrical plug molding with bulb adapters and a rheostat for mood control.

A bright backdrop of peach-colored paint provides an extra measure of pizzazz for the setting. Also inventive is the old restaurant table base topped with a piece of vinyl-covered plywood.

This contemporary paper lantern light fixture is a snap to make. Taking your cue from the illustration *below,* cut five lengths of 2x2s to proper size, make notches in the crosspieces with a saw and chisel, and drill holes for the round lamp cord. Screw the 2x2s together, then glue on brackets for support. Run the cord (with a line switch) over the top of the frame, then down the upright to a wall outlet.

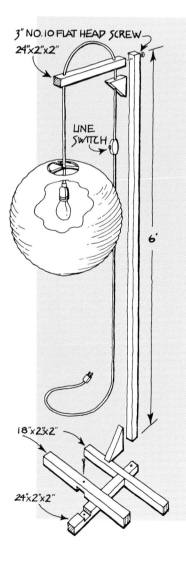

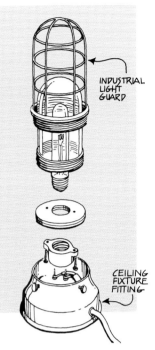

INDUSTRIAL LIGHT GUARD

CEILING FIXTURE FITTING

A shelf light similar to this one, *above,* can be made at low cost and with minimal do-it-yourself expertise. Its components include a metal industrial light guard from a hardware store and a ceiling fixture fitting from a lamp shop. For best results, first buy the light guard, then look for a ceiling fixture that will fit the guard's base. Wire as shown in the illustration, *above right,* then fit with a showcase bulb.

Show off your favorite plants or accessories with an atmospheric display light like this one, *left.*

To make a similar lamp, cut wood pieces from 1x12-inch cedar boards. Groove two edges to accept a square of translucent plastic, and screw a wired ceramic socket to the wood surface opposite the plastic. Glue and clamp together all of the wood pieces except the bottom section. Drill a hole in the side of the lamp and install the cord and switch. Glue ¼x¼-inch strips of wood ¾ inch from the bottom edge of the lamp. Set a mini spot bulb in the socket and screw the bottom in place.

To use this lamp as an uplight, simply turn it horizontally. The light will shine upward at a 45-degree angle

Reminiscent of designs popular during the Art Deco era, this table lamp would make a nice addition to any contemporary decor. The shiny metal cluster that forms the vertical section of the lamp is made from 1-inch-round chrome-plated shower rods, cut to a variety of lengths. To make the base, cut rods in the following amounts and lengths: two 12-inch, two 14-inch, two 16-inch, two 18-inch, and one 24-inch. With the tallest rod in the center, arrange the rods to form a cluster, keeping all bottom ends flush. Secure the cluster in place with epoxy glue; let dry.

Cut a base to the desired size from a 2-inch-thick pine board. Center rods on the pine piece; trace around the group with a pencil. Chisel out the assembly area to a ¼-inch depth. Drill a hole centered directly beneath the position of the longest rod. Chisel a channel on the underside of the base for the cord clearance. Position rods in the base; secure the longest rod with a lamp pipe. Add the harp, wiring, and your choice of shade, and the lamp is ready to plug in.

Transform any ordinary wire lampshade with this colorful "glad rag" fabric treatment. Just rip 44-inch-wide fabric remnants into 3-inch-wide strips. Then—beginning at the bottom of the lampshade base—weave the sections of fabric over and under the spokes, wrapping each strip around each spoke as you work; tack the pieces in place. For the best results, use a shade frame with an uneven number of spokes.

This good-looking lamp base is a project to make in your workshop. Cut out a series of seven oak plywood circles, ranging from 6 to 12 inches in diameter, and edge each circle with compatible veneer tape. Center a hole in each circle for wiring, and drill three more evenly spaced holes. Insert the threaded metal rods through the three holes and secure each disk with washers and nuts. Add the socket and wiring. Choose a lampshade that is proportionate in size to the lamp base.

An hour or two is all you'll need to create a contemporary track light like this one, *right*. The inexpensive fixture consists of nothing more than two yellow-enameled reflector lamps clamped to a metal shower rod. A 1-inch-square rod was cut to fit a 60-inch-long frame made of pine 1x4s. (The frame consists of three pieces: a back and two sides.) These lamps come ready-made with mounting clamps and curly electrical cords. Unpainted, shiny metal versions also are available. Once assembled, the handy track system can be mounted on any flat surface, horizontally or vertically.

A young child is sure to love this delightful nursery night-light, *right*. To make the friendly 42-inch-tall bird, first enlarge the pattern shown *below*. Using ¼-inch hardboard, cut two wings and two body shapes. Next, cut a

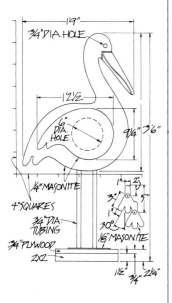

6-inch circle in the body as shown, and drill a ¾-inch-diameter hole for the eyes in each body piece. Cut the feet from ⅛-inch hardboard.

Build a 12x12-inch base from 2x2s; top with a square of ¾-inch plywood. Next, secure two 2x2 crosspieces to receive the ¾-inch-diameter legs. Cut one 20-inch leg from a wood dowel; cut the other from tubing to house the wiring. Top each leg with 1½-inch-thick wood blocks. Screw a porcelain fixture to the blocks; finish the wiring.

Using ¾-inch-thick scrap lumber, block the wings away from the body pieces, centering over cutouts. Glue and screw body pieces to the top of the legs; block the remainder of the body pieces so that both halves are parallel.

To finish, paint the body white inside and out, the beak orange, and the base and details black.

Memories of childhood are apt to arise when you make this contemporary "stack of sticks" light fixture. With glue and 12-inch lengths of screen molding in hand, you simply stack (and glue) the wooden pieces (in Lincoln-log fashion) until the square column measures 24 inches high.

Designed to be placed on the floor or on a shelf as a decorative "mood" light, the column is stabilized with a 12-inch-square plywood base. The base also houses a porcelain light socket, wiring, and a floodlight lamp bulb.

Artful Ideas

chapter 14

Furniture alone does not make a room noteworthy. When all is said and done, it's the seemingly small touches that have the biggest impact on a decorating scheme. Happily, it doesn't cost a lot to create a memorable decor. Art and accessories are infinite in their variety, and in their price ranges, too. Indeed, as you may have already discovered, some of the nicest finishing touches are free.

How you choose to accent your home is an entirely personal matter. As with furnishings, finishing touches run the gamut from formal to informal, traditional to contemporary, and all variations in between. What matters most is that accessories reflect your personality.

Left, a magnificent heirloom quilt adorns the wall of this understated dining area. To give the quilt its due as the star of the setting, the number of objects in front of it have been strictly limited in both number and size. Rather than detract from the presence of the quilt, the bowl of pears and the flower-filled vase accentuate its eye-catching beauty.

Anything goes when it comes to accessories—as long as the objects are pleasing to look at and have meaning to you. The vignette above features a collection of old checkerboards informally hung on the wall. The grouping is arranged so that the smaller boards balance the larger ones. Anchoring the arrangement is a century-old chest topped with antique toleware and a whimsical folk art rabbit.

Shown here is a novel and easy way to recycle pretty gift wrapping paper. From a single sheet of paper, cut three identical motifs, separating the design elements from the background. Leave the fourth design uncut. To begin, glue the uncut design to a piece of cardboard. Dab small drops of clear silicone cement on the motif (see photo, *left*).

Position corresponding segments of the second motif on top of the glue. Let dry, then repeat the procedure twice, stacking motifs for a three-dimensional effect. For a rounded look, roll edges of leaves and petals around a pencil, curling them slightly before setting them on the glue. Lastly, brush on decoupage glaze, then frame.

Artwork is all the more meaningful when it's created by you or a member of your family. Pictured *at right* is a collection of torn-paper masterpieces that is fun and simple to create. In a single evening, you and your fellow artists can fill an entire wall with thrifty masterpieces—all originals.

The only materials you need are origami paper or other high-quality fadeless papers (available at art stores), mat boards, white glue, and simple frames.

From a variety of papers, tear rectangles, squares, and circular shapes to make simple floral, fruit, or abstract compositions. Arrange the torn shapes on a piece of background paper (creating whatever design you want), then glue the pieces in place. Mount your finished piece behind a window of mat board, then frame.

Patience, not talent, is the only thing you need to create a dramatic wrapping-paper wall hanging like the one pictured *at left*.

To make your own eye-catching wall hanging, simply cut vari-shaped pieces from an assortment of colorful gift wrapping papers or wallpaper remnants, then use rubber cement to attach the pieces to a sheet of hardboard or corrugated cardboard. For real impact, consider using the same technique on an entire wall.

Store-bought frames are generally best for artwork, but family portraits can be framed less formally. These just-for-fun fabric frames, *right,* are every bit as personal as the pictures they embrace. They're made from men's handkerchiefs stitched into tubes, stuffed with polyester fiber, and sewn together at the corners. (This seven-piece gallery required only seven handkerchiefs, but if you prefer, use fabric scraps.) Cardboard, sandwiched between two layers of felt sewn to the back of the frame, provides a rigid backing.

If you can sew on a button, you can make this countrified cross-stitch sampler. It's that easy. Use a medium-to-heavyweight fabric that is 1½ yards long and 54 inches wide, and has an even, loose weave (counting the threads is the hardest part). Stretch and staple the fabric around a 1x2 frame, or use artist's stretcher bars. Use a medium-weight yarn to make the ⅜-inch stitches (eight cross-stitches equal 3 inches, which is the height of these letters).

This design is 93 stitches wide, from the C on "confronted" to the H on "with" (including spaces between letters). The size of the sampler (before framing) measures 40 by 50 inches.

You can easily and inexpensively beautify a wall by creating a patchwork wall hanging like this one, *opposite.* The idea is to select a favorite scene from a postcard, snapshot, or slide, then re-create the scene with fabric.

Begin by gathering up the following materials: backing fabric of your choice, bits and pieces of fabric remnants for landscape patterns, upholstery gimp (or decorative trim) for outlining the landscape patterns, fusible webbing, fabric glue, and enough 4-inch-wide fabric to make a border.

To make your own scenic pattern, simply project your favorite slide onto brown paper and trace the outlines with a pen or pencil. Or, if you don't have a slide, draw a grid across a snapshot or other picture, then enlarge the grid sections on a sheet of paper.

The next step is to transfer the pattern to the backing fabric. To do this, first lay sheets of fusible webbing over the entire backing fabric, and pin it in place along the margins. Cut apart the brown paper pattern, then cut shapes from the fabric scraps. Lay the pieces carefully on the webbing-covered background. When the pieces are in place, cover with a press cloth and carefully press the entire hanging on the front side. Remove pins; press again on the front and back.

To finish, glue strips of gimp or other decorative trim over all raw edges. Next, glue strips of 4-inch-wide fabric to the edges of the hanging. Fold the raw edge to the back and glue again. Attach fabric loops for hanging.

These days, it's not uncommon for a picture frame to cost considerably more than the artwork. If you've been hanging on to odds-and-ends art items for fear that framing will cost too much, here, *above,* is a handsome money-saving solution.

The "frame" for this 1904 sheet-music cover consists of nothing more than a piece of ⅛-inch-thick glass and a piece of ⅛-inch-thick particle-board. The sheet music is centered on a piece of blue construction paper (thus eliminating the need for a mat), and sandwiched between the glass and particleboard. Holding the frame together are "Swiss clips" from an art store. They're the little chrome fingers you barely see at the edges of the glass (see drawing *at right).*

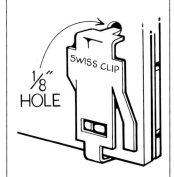

There's no need to go to an art gallery to obtain interesting art for your home. With minimal expertise you can create your own. The original three-dimensional "art" pictured *at right* looks like a modern painting, but actually the medium is fabric, not oil.

The eye-catching graphic consists of three fabric-covered wooden frames (two triangles and a rectangle), made of ½x1½-inch boards purchased at a lumber store. The fabric is simply stretched taut and stapled to the back side of the frames.

Ordinary picture hooks are all you need to hang the lightweight fabric art on the wall. Here a dark-painted background emphasizes the fabric graphic and the trio of ceramic masks.

Here's another idea for do-it-yourself artwork. These "paintings," *left,* are nothing more than pieces of lace glued to colored illustration board. Almost anything will work—handkerchiefs, doilies, place mats, even part of an old dress. Check out antique shops, garage sales, and secondhand stores for good prospects. Or, if you're artistically inclined, use scissors to cut your own intricate designs from paper.

To make your own, first cut illustration board to size with a matting knife. Next, dot a little white glue on the lace (or whatever) with a toothpick, then press onto the board until dry. These "instant" acrylic frames came from an art supply store.

Hanging pictures in a pleasing arrangement is like fitting together a puzzle: if one piece is out of place, the grouping doesn't work.

One way to tie your artwork together is to have at least one straight line running through the grouping. In the room above, a nice wall composition was formed by aligning five of the eight framed prints on a single base line. The three remaining prints are hung pyramid-style around the central key print. Note the height of the base line: it's almost even with the top of the upholstered chair.

Here's a clever framing idea. Four companionable museum prints, *left,* are placed together in a single frame. In addition to eliminating the need for four separate frames, the all-in-one placement gives the small prints a greater sense of visual importance by being grouped in close proximity.

To create an interesting illusion, a piece of wallpaper to match the covering on the wall was used as the matting for the prints.

PICTURE-HANGING TIPS

- **Hang pieces at eye level** or below. If you will be looking at the art most often from a seated position (as is the case in most living rooms), hang it at seated eye level. The biggest mistake most people make is to hang their artwork too high on the wall. In a tiered grouping, place the central units at eye level.
- **Vary the shapes** in a grouping for the most interesting composition. For instance, you could include both rectangular and square frames, not just one or the other.
- **Don't hang pictures too close together** or too far apart. The space between two pictures shouldn't be greater than the width of a single picture. (For instance, place two 10-inch-wide prints less than 10 inches apart.)
- **Always think of the grouping as a whole,** not as a series of separate entities. Also, consider the size of the artwork in relation to the size (height and width) of the wall. One or two small pictures on a vast expanse of wall will look ridiculously out of scale—so will a large picture placed on a small wall.
- **Consider the kinship** of objects to one another and to the background. Delicate watercolors will be overwhelmed if placed next to strong oils or bold graphics. Similarly, colorful artwork is apt to look muted if placed against a patterned or equally colorful background. Wide, solid-color mats or frames help paintings stand out from patterned walls.
- **Strive for balance.** When you hang artwork above a sofa, table, or chair, make sure the piece of furniture is of equal or greater visual weight than the art.

There are any number of ways to put artwork on display. This large contemporary poster, *above,* though framed conventionally, is hung in a rather "far-out" manner.

The poster is placed several inches from the wall, giving it a three-dimensional look. It appears to be suspended in midair. The secret to creating a similar effect is to hang the picture with monofilament fishing line attached to screw hooks in the ceiling.

We don't recommend that you hang artwork over a heat register or radiator. The radiator pictured here is old and nonfunctional.

An art wall doesn't have to be expensive to be interesting. *At right,* a pride of old picture frames salvaged from flea markets and garage sales turns a collection of pear prints into a mini-gallery. Although the frames appear at first glance to be randomly placed, the asymmetrical arrangement is roughly rectangular, with six prints pivoting around a central frame. Within the geometric unit, several sizes and shapes of frames are used. Note how the small yellow antiqued chest anchors the grouping and picks up the colors of the pear prints.

If, like most people, you're a collector of many things, but of nothing in particular, try placing your accessories in small vignettes. In decorative terms, "vignettes" are visually pleasing groups of objects characterized by compactness, subtlety, and, sometimes, wit. In other words, be selective with what you choose to display. Resist the temptation to go overboard with an abundance of things.

The vignette pictured *above* contains an assortment of disparate but eye-pleasing objects, artfully arranged on an antique dresser.

When it comes to creating a warm and personal living environment, nothing can take the place of accessories. *Any* object, as long as it has meaning for you, is worthy of display. This doesn't mean, however, that you should put all of your possessions on parade. Collections are more likely to be appreciated when they include only your favorite or most striking examples.

Proof that accessories need not be fancy to be *effective* is the china cupboard, *above left*. It's filled, not with fine china, but with a garden variety of colored glass as vivid and various as a bouquet of spring flowers.

You can use just about any utilitarian item as a just-for-fun *objet d'art. At left,* an assortment of old, clear light bulbs with their filaments intact makes for an "enlightened" tabletop display.

Look for unusual old bulbs at antique shops or secondhand stores. Check out old lamps for bulbs with their filaments still intact. If you can't locate any old-fashioned bulbs, commercial display bulbs will work nicely, too. These bulbs are mounted in heavy porcelain display sockets (available at lamp shops and hardware stores).

For a pleasing *effect,* try placing clear bulbs on a windowsill. They'll sparkle whenever the sun shines.

Collections can consist of virtually anything. And most collections—be they fancy or just-for-fun—can be assimilated into a decorating scheme. The point is, don't be shy about showing off your handiwork, your hobby, or your favorite collections. Let your unique personality and sense of style rub off on your surroundings.

Here, a cuddly assortment of teddy bears, lovingly collected over the years, never fails to catch the attention of guests and put smiles on their faces. Each bear was chosen for its unique facial expression, and all are happily housed in old wicker baskets. Every now and then, the owner singles out one of the bears for special attention on the sofa.

This homeowner's accessory collection doesn't stop with bears. Other favorite finds are proudly displayed on a pedestal table. The dried flowers are changed in accordance with the season.

Money-Saving Storage

chapter

15

Storage—or better said, *lack* of it—is a perennial problem in most households. And, despite the best efforts to pare down and weed out, our possessions continue to proliferate. If you'd like to improve the storage situation at your house, try one or more of these practical, do-it-yourself solutions.

An off-the-wall approach to storage is a good idea if you're short of table or floor space. This lattice-backed shelving system is designed to hold stereo equipment, tape cassettes, and record albums in an orderly, easy-to-reach fashion. The 24-inch-wide lattice molding strips are attached with brads to an 8-foot-tall pine frame (see the illustration, *opposite*).

Chair braces and ⅛-inch steel cable (purchased from a sailboat dealer) support the 18-inch-deep shelves. Have the boat shop cut the cable to size and make the eyes (loops on the end) with their machine. Leave out a lattice strip behind each shelf until you've run connecting wires to the stereo components. By placing the shelf unit in front of a wall outlet, you can neatly hide all the power cords behind the lattice framework.

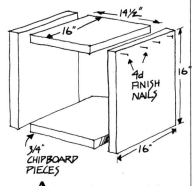

3/4" CHIPBOARD PIECES

14½"

16"

16"

4d FINISH NAILS

16"

A basic cube is one of the most versatile and flexible storage pieces around. Stack and arrange the open-ended cubes pictured here in any configuration you want—they're ultra-simple to make. Using the diagram *above* as your guide, buy chipboard from a lumberyard and have it cut to size. Glue the pieces together with white glue and secure with fourpenny finishing nails, as shown. Paint the cubes, or leave them natural.

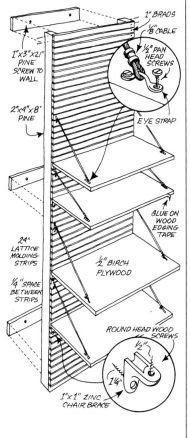

1" BRADS
⅛" CABLE
1"x3"x21" PINE SCREW TO WALL
½" PAN HEAD SCREWS
EYE STRAP
2"x4"x8' PINE
GLUE ON WOOD EDGING TAPE
24" LATTICE MOLDING STRIPS
½" BIRCH PLYWOOD
¼" SPACE BETWEEN STRIPS
ROUND HEAD WOOD SCREWS
½"
1¼"
1"x1" ZINC CHAIR BRACE

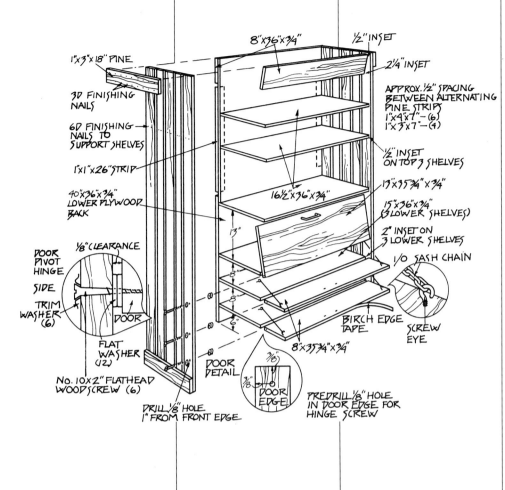

Materials List:
Lumber:
Note: If possible, have the lumberyard cut as specified.
2 pine 1x1s (36 inches long)
4 pine 1x3s (7 feet long)
6 pine 1x4s (7 feet long)
4 pine 1x3s (18 inches long)
1 36x45¾x⅛-inch hardboard panel
From two 4x8-foot sheets of ¾-inch knotty pine plywood, cut:
2 doors, 35¾x8 inches
1 door, 35¾x13 inches
2 top braces, 36x8 inches
3 shelves, 16½x36 inches
3 shelves, 15x36 inches
1 lower-back panel, 36x40 inches

Hardware:
6 No.10x2-inch screws with trim washers
12 flat washers; 12 screw eyes
1 lb. 6d finishing nails
8-foot sash chain
3 door handles
1 roll ¾-inch birch plywood edge tape

This attractive knotty pine storage unit holds and displays all manner of stereo equipment and paraphernalia. In addition to providing a level, nonvibrating surface for a turntable, the spacious cabi-

net offers plenty of "breathing room" for a variety of other components.

The open shelves are placed at just the right height so that the dials, lights, and switches are easy to see and reach. The lower three shelves are tailored for record and tape storage, plus miscellaneous gear. The only visible wires are those running to the speakers. All others run through holes drilled in the back panel.

Step-by-Step Directions
1. Taking your cues from the illustration *above,* first assemble the side panels. Alternate three 1x4s and two 1x3s (the seven footers) for each side. Then, nail and glue an 18-inch, 1x3 cleat to the top and bottom of each panel.

2. Once you've completed the sides, nail and glue on a lower-back panel of plywood (the top panel comes later). Then install the lower four shelves. Be sure to space the shelves so that the doors will fit properly.

3. You can now stand the unit in an upright position to complete the rest of the project. Attach the rear-top brace, then nail and glue a 1x1 strip to each rear edge between the top brace and the lower-back panel. Next, nail and glue the top-back panel to the inside edge of the two strips.

Install the front-top brace as shown in the illustration. Before you install the other two shelves, figure out where you want to place the stereo equipment so that the dials are easy to reach. For best results, measure the height and width of each component

(with all the lids open). Make sure the tallest component on each shelf has an inch of headroom, then nail and glue in the shelves.

4. The final step is to install the doors for the lower three shelves. The hinges are simply screws and washers. Sash chain and screw eyes hold the open doors flat for a handy horizontal surface.

Once the doors are in place, attach metal or plastic handles as shown. Glue birch plywood edging tape to the exposed plywood edges. For a professional look, countersink all nails and fill the holes with wood putty.

How you finish the piece is a matter of personal preference. You can stain and finish the cabinet with polyurethane varnish, use an oil finish, or—easiest of all—leave the piece in its natural state.

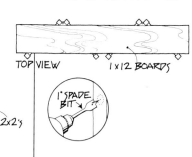

This simple, foldable shelf unit consists of four "ladders" hinged together with pine boards resting on dowel-rod rungs. To make the unit, you'll need a drill with a 1-inch spade bit and the following materials:
- 8 pine 2x2s, cut the length you want the uprights
- 20 one-inch dowel rods, 18 inches long
- 5 pine 1x12s for shelves
- 6 hinges (2½ or 3 inches in size)

Here's how to assemble the unit: First, drill 1-inch holes halfway through the pine uprights. Then, secure the dowel rods in the holes with white glue. Finally, join the ladder pieces together with hinges, as shown in the illustration *above*.

Organize your life—or at least your bills and other correspondence—with this handy desk-top shelf unit, *left*. It's made entirely of birch-faced plywood and fits across the top of almost any desk. You'll find it's a great way to rid your desk of clutter while keeping frequently used materials close at hand.

The unit shown here measures 28x18x6 inches, but you can adjust the finished size to accommodate various desk supplies.

The opening on the right measures 12 inches high, the pigeonholes are 4 inches high, and the horizontal slots are 6 inches high. Leave the top lefthand side uncovered to facilitate the use of a lamp. To assemble, glue and nail the plywood pieces together.

By building this grow-light shelf unit, you'll provide a home not only for books, but for favorite plants as well. Leave room at the top of the unit for a spacious plant shelf; then, add a built-in fixture to supply plenty of light.

Use 1x10-inch pine boards for the shelves, sides, bottom, and top. The back section is a 4x6-foot piece of ½-inch plywood that's nailed in place to the top and sides of the unit.

Run adjustable metal shelving strips along the sides for shelf supports. Space the shelves at desired heights to hold accessories and books of various sizes.

Install a two-tube fluorescent fixture at the top of the unit; conceal the fixture with a 1x4-inch pine fascia.

Paint the finished unit or, for a natural look, use a clear wood sealer. To protect the wood from water spills, add an extra coat or two of sealer to the plant shelf.

This costly looking, country French armoire can be yours for the price of a plain-Jane ready-made wardrobe closet (from an unfinished furniture store) and a product called "cabinet overlay molding."

Begin the transformation process by nailing two 1x3 verticals on each side of the wardrobe. Then nail lengths of 1½-inch corner molding along the left and right front edges. Extend the corner molding three inches above the top of the cabinet so it will cover the corners of the crown later. Next, add the Queen Anne-style legs.

If possible, remove the doors and work on the floor. First, frame the door with a decorative molding. Miter the corners and use 1-inch finishing nails. Fill joints and nail holes with matching wood putty, then sand smooth.

The fancy designs on the doors are made with ⅝-inch-wide cabinet overlay molding, including ready-made reversible arcs, straight pieces, and embossed wood carvings available at most building supply stores. Cut the straight pieces with a coping saw and use the reversible arcs for right or left angles as your design requires. Nail the molding to the door with 1-inch finishing nails and use more wood putty to mask nail holes and joints. Attach the embossed wood carvings wherever you want them. Position the keyhole plates, mark and drill holes for keys, and screw on plates.

The crown is a box made of 1x6 lumber—with lots of added trim—that sits atop the wardrobe. Cut the cove molding and miter the front corners. Screw the three pieces of cove molding to three pieces of 1x2. Drill several holes along the bottom edge of each 1x2; attach the 1x2 to the inside of the 1x6 box with flathead wood screws. Just below the cove molding, nail on one strip of ½-inch scrollwork molding, one strip of block pattern molding, and another strip of scrollwork.

Nail on an embossed wood carving, centered over the doors and the two embossed fans. Then place the crown on top of the cabinet. Sand all rough spots, then stain and varnish to get the finish you want.

Materials List:
- 1 unfinished wardrobe with doors
- 4 1x3s for vertical trim on sides
- 1½-inch corner molding for front edges
- 4 screw-in Queen Anne-style legs
- Matching wood putty

For doors:
- 8 pieces door molding to frame doors
- Embossed wood carvings—wings, circles, oblongs, fleurettes
- 2 brass-plated keyholes with keys

For crown:
- 2 1x6s for sides
- 2 1x6s for front and back
- 3 pieces cove molding
- 2 pieces ½-inch scrollwork molding
- 1 piece 2-inch block pattern molding
- 1 embossed carving over doors
- 2 embossed wood fans
- One-inch finishing nails
- 1¼-inch flathead wood screws

Tools: Coping saw, saber saw or handsaw, drill, hammer, screwdriver, fine sandpaper, miter box.

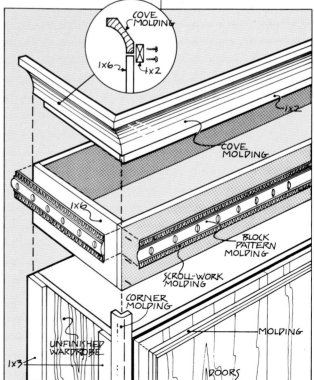

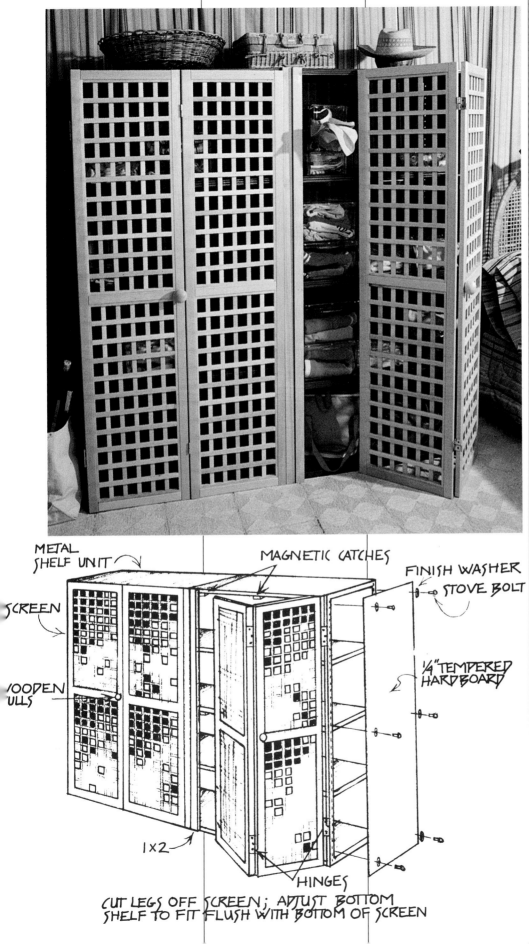

METAL
SHELF UNIT

SCREEN

WOODEN
PULLS

1x2

MAGNETIC CATCHES

FINISH WASHER
STOVE BOLT

¼" TEMPERED
HARDBOARD

HINGES

CUT LEGS OFF SCREEN; ADJUST BOTTOM
SHELF TO FIT FLUSH WITH BOTTOM OF SCREEN

Metal utility shelving (also known as industrial shelving) is most often found in basements and garages. Properly camouflaged, however, these inexpensive shelf units make excellent storage "dressers" for the bedroom.

Materials List:
- 2 shelving units (any size)
- 4 lattice screen doors (cut the size of the shelving units)
- 2 pieces ¼-inch hardboard (sized to cover ends)
- 8 hinges
- 4 magnetic catches
- 1 1x2 (cut to the height of shelf unit)
- 6 nuts and bolts
- Paint

Instructions:
Assemble the shelf units according to the manufacturer's directions, then bolt the units together along the uprights. Trim the tops and sides of the decorative door panels to size. Hinge two of the door panels together as shown, then hinge the connected doors to the shelf uprights. When doors are secured, adjust the fit by planing or sanding the edges.

Camouflage the ends of the shelf units by bolting on a piece of hardboard to each exposed end. If the shelves are to be used to hold heavy items, stabilize the back by adding a piece of hardboard to the back of the units.

Sand all edges of hardboard and doors, and paint as desired. Install magnetic catch hardware.

Easy to build, this handy, see-through storage stand can be put to good use in a kitchen, hallway, or bathroom. The stand measures 1 foot square and 30 inches high. Make the 12x11½-inch shelves from ½-inch plywood cut to 12x1¾-inch strips and joined with resin glue.

Sand and fill the exposed wood edges and apply two coats of clear shellac. For the sides, cut two pieces of ¼-inch acrylic and smooth the edges with sandpaper. Drill pilot holes for 2½-inch-long screws and assemble the unit.

This slanted, open-bin storage unit is designed to hold a miscellany of items—books, magazines, toys, yarns, and other odds and ends that need a home of their own.

Cut the 12-inch-deep shelves and the frame from ½-inch plywood. The outer dimensions measure 55x33 inches. Assemble the shelves with slip joints at 12½-inch intervals. Paint or stain the storage piece the color of your choice.

Looking for ways to squeeze more storage space from your kitchen or pantry? Don't overlook the versatility (and low cost) of perforated hardboard. Think beyond the usual pots-and-pans routine: All manner of brackets, hooks, and shelf supports are available (at hardware stores and lumberyards) to hold myriad kitchen utensils.

For additional storage, use stackable, plastic drawer units that you top with a sturdy pine work surface. The drawers are convenient for storing and organizing gadgets, recipes, plastic bags, dish towels, and a telephone book.

Most of us, when we've run out of places to stash things, tend to forget about overhead space. So unless you're uncommonly tall (or your ceilings are uncommonly low) don't forget to look up the next time you're searching for extra storage.

This overhead storage ledge is designed to hold lots of lightweight but bulky possessions. Build the ledge by nailing 1x2 cleats to the wall, preassembling the edge strip and plywood shelf, then screwing the plywood to the bottoms of the cleats. Finish by nailing both ends of the edge strip into the ends of the side cleats. Paint the ledge to match your decor.

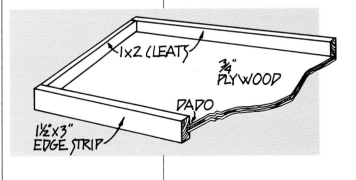

Penny-Pinching Projects

chapter

16

A basic knowledge of carpentry techniques will take you a long way toward saving money. More often than not, a piece of furniture made by you is going to cost less than the store-bought equivalent. But extra savings aside, there's also a feeling of pride and accomplishment that comes from making your own furniture. Whatever your motive, the projects in this chapter are sure to please.

Purchased in a store, an upholstered "island" bed could easily cost you $1,000. For much, much less you can build your own freestanding sleep unit. This versatile, contemporary island bed features a built-in headboard and its own electrical outlets.

With the springs and mattress on the floor, build a 1x12 U-shaped frame around both sides and the foot of the bed, then nail the frame to the bookcase-headboard made of more 1x12s and ¾-inch plywood. Add electrical outlets to each side of the headboard and drill two holes on top for the lamps. To upholster the bed unit, you'll need carpet remnants, glue, and a staple gun.

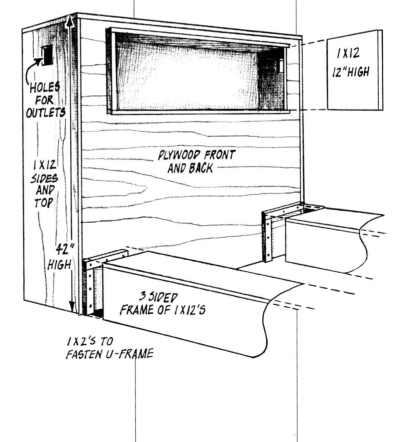

HOLES FOR OUTLETS

1 X 12 SIDES AND TOP

42" HIGH

1 X 2'S TO FASTEN U-FRAME

3 SIDED FRAME OF 1 X 12'S

PLYWOOD FRONT AND BACK

1 X 12 12" HIGH

This built-in banquette is designed for seating, sleeping, and storage purposes. The unit consists of four plywood boxes screwed together—two large ones for the base, two smaller boxes for the backrest. Boards nailed to the front make a lip to keep the 5-inch-thick foam cushions from slipping off the ledge.

Using the diagram, *right*, as your guide, build the boxes to fit, wall to wall. Or, if you prefer, build one freestanding section with wood strips on all the exposed sides. Heavy-duty fabric such as canvas or duck is your best bet for the box-type slipcovers.

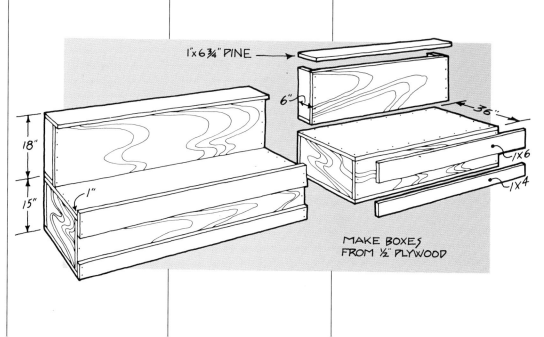

This cushy, pillowy platform sofa is an easy-to-build, low-cost version of an expensive European-style look.

A 54x75-inch full-size mattress (covered with a quilted bedspread) tops the wooden platform. Upholstery over the exposed parts of the base is made from ½-inch foam and fabric to match the spread. The backrest is nothing more than a pile of pillows.

Building the two 18x36-inch box bases is a simple matter of nailing together 1x10s (see drawing). The plywood platform takes a little more work. Since plywood comes only in 48-inch widths, you'll have to splice on a 1x8, lengthwise, to get the proper support for the mattress. Round off all four corners (3-inch radius) with a saber saw.

For extra depth, nail and glue 1x2s (as shown) around the perimeter of the platform (use a rounded piece of a 1x4 under each corner).

Tack or staple ½-inch-thick foam around the sides of the boxes and the edges of the platform. Finish by covering the foam sections with lengths of fabric.

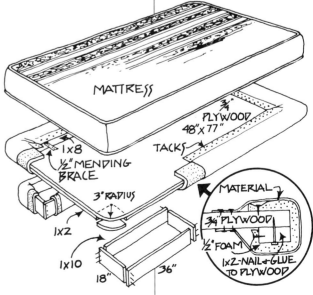

MATTRESS

PLYWOOD 48"x77"

3"

TACKS

1x8

½" MENDING BRACE

MATERIAL

3" RADIUS

¾ PLYWOOD

½" FOAM

1x2

1x2-NAIL-GLUE TO PLYWOOD

1x10

18"

36"

Hidden assets are part of the bargain when you build this contemporary seating platform and complementary coffee table, *left*. The sofa seats three, sleeps one, serves drinks to a crowd, and stores odds-and-ends in its hidden holds. The sofa project requires two and one-half 4x8 sheets of inexpensive ¾-inch plywood, about 25 feet of 1x2s, lots of 1¼-inch wood screws and 1½-inch finishing nails, and enough carpet to cover the finished piece. The end table/liquor cabinet and the rectangular seating platform are really two separate pieces bolted together (*see* diagram, *below*). Divide the long box into two equal compartments, nail a partition in place, and cut two trap doors to fit over the openings. Use a utility knife to cut the carpet, then glue and staple it to the boxes.

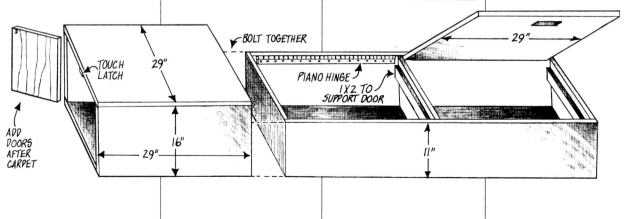

ADD DOORS AFTER CARPET

TOUCH LATCH

29"

16"

29"

BOLT TOGETHER

PIANO HINGE

1X2 TO SUPPORT DOOR

29"

11"

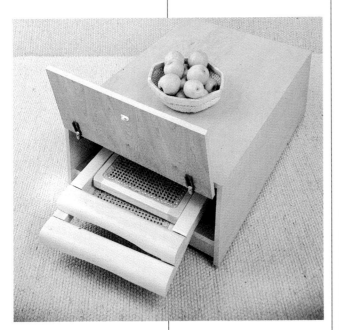

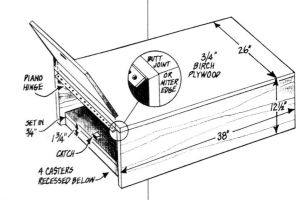

The rectangular coffee table, *left*, doubles as a storage cabinet for several folding chairs. Have your lumberyard cut ¾-inch birch plywood to your specifications, then build a basic box or rectangle as per the illustration *above*. Use either a piano hinge or Selby hinges (as shown in the photo) for the lift-up door.

A piece of ¼-inch-thick glass protects the surface of the carpeted storage/end table, *below*. For best results, carpet the sides and top of the cube before you cut and install the oak doors. For a sleek look, use piano hinges and touch latches on the doors instead of knobs.

The two under-the-cushion storage compartments (see the diagram, *opposite page*) are perfect for stowing sheets, blankets, and pillows. The hatch-style doors are supported by 1x2 braces screwed onto the front and sides of each compartment. Piano hinges along the back edges make access easy.

Built from sturdy 2½-inch pine dowels, this handsome four-poster bed makes a big statement with simple materials and design. Based on a grid system, the bed consists of three rectangular frames hitched together on four uprights. The bottom frames are braced by short dowels.

To simplify the project, have your local lumberyard cut all the dowels to length. Use 5-inch stove bolts (¼ inch in diameter) to fasten the three frames and attach them to the uprights. Drill holes as shown, *below,* and countersink the bolts. (Line up the holes so the bolts fit.)

Secure the short dowels (1½-inch diameter) with 4-inch stove bolts (¼-inch diameter). Screw in 6-foot sections of angle iron on the long sides of the bed. For the bed board, cut two pieces of plywood 26x54 inches and 48x54 inches. The long dowels at the side of the bed extend several inches past the mattress. To fill this space (and keep the pillows from slipping) build a shelf from a 60-inch 1x6 board. Cut the board to fit around the dowels and lie flat. For the canopy, hem and drape mosquito netting or other light fabric.

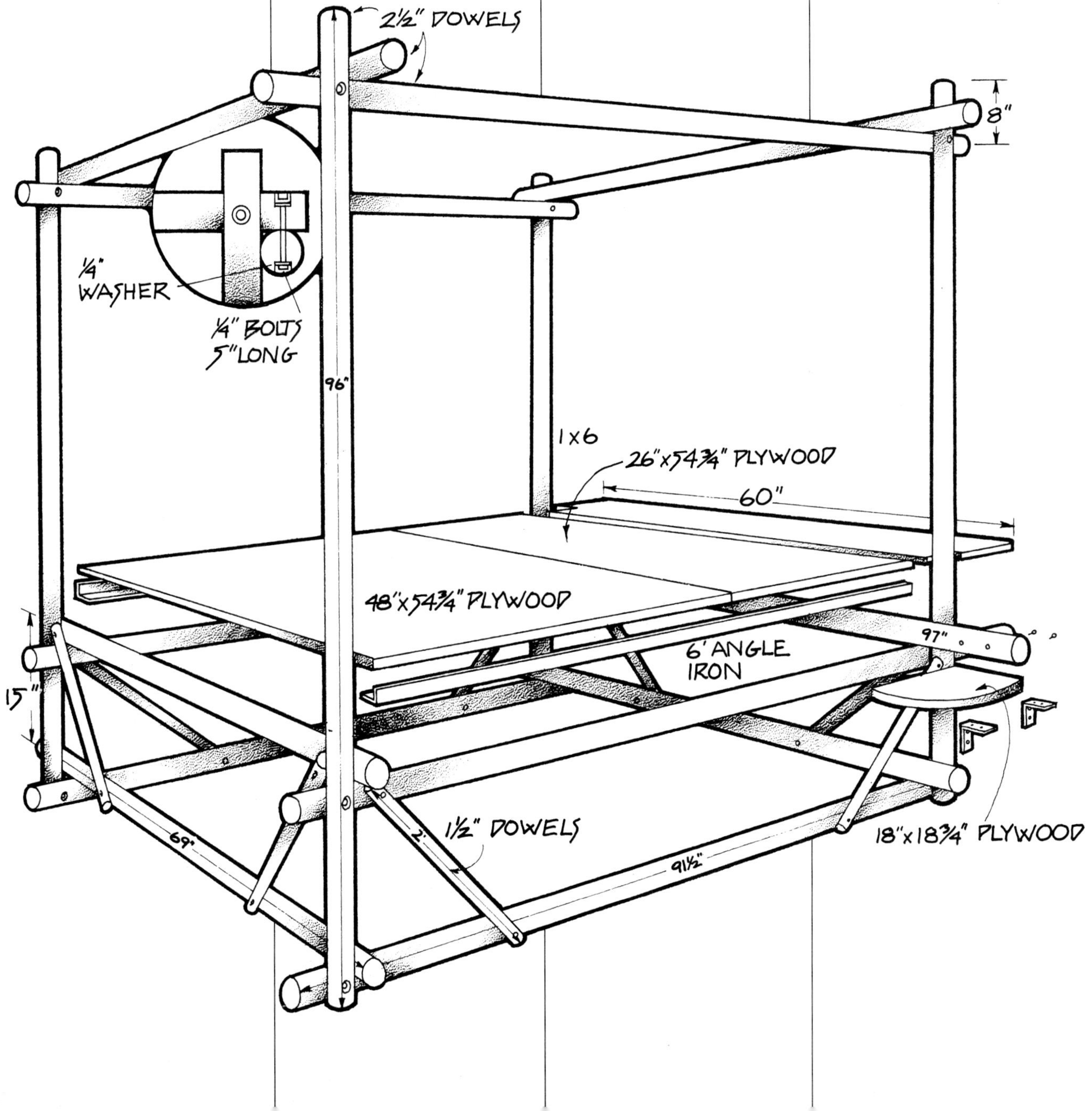

2½" DOWELS

8"

¼" WASHER

¼" BOLTS 5"LONG

96"

1x6

26"x54¾" PLYWOOD

60"

48"x54¾" PLYWOOD

6' ANGLE IRON

97"

15"

1½" DOWELS

18"x18¾" PLYWOOD

69"

91½"

THE DYER'S ART
ikat, batik, plangi

If your house or apartment lacks a separate dining room, or—worse yet—a place to put a dining table, here's a thrifty solution that's sure to save the day.

A two-in-one table, *left* and *above*, serves as a space-saving wall console most of the time, but quickly turns into a spacious, stylish dining table whenever needed.

To make the table, start with a store-bought Parsons table (this one was purchased unfinished), then add a hinged flip-flop top as shown in the diagram *at right*.

The top consists of two pieces of 2x4-foot birch plywood (¾-inch thick) precut and hinged to fit the 24x48-inch dimensions of the table.

The edges of the plywood are finished with wood tape and painted with semigloss enamel to match the table itself.

When it's time to dine, simply pull the table away from the wall, unfold the flip top, turn it 90 degrees, and *voilà!* you have a 48-inch-square surface that seats up to eight people.

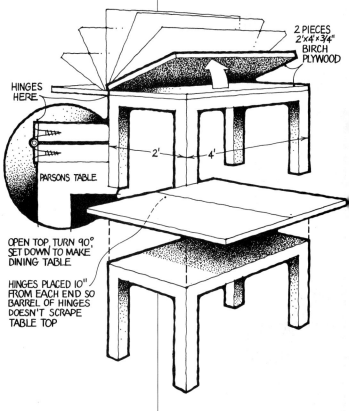

2 PIECES
2'x4'x¾"
BIRCH
PLYWOOD

HINGES
HERE

PARSONS TABLE

2'

4'

OPEN TOP, TURN 90°
SET DOWN TO MAKE
DINING TABLE

HINGES PLACED 10"
FROM EACH END SO
BARREL OF HINGES
DOESN'T SCRAPE
TABLE TOP

In just a matter of hours, you can transform almost any old four-panel door into a terrific table base like this one, *right*. Although the procedure will vary according to the design of the panels, the following information should give you a general idea of how to go about making your own table.

First, trim the door to standard dining table height (29 inches), then strip it with good paint remover and sandpaper, or have it "dipped" by a professional furniture stripper. With a four-panel door like this one, use a circular saw to cut the door into three parts, as shown.

Find and mark the center of the longest part of the door, then make a notch in the raised portions (on both sides) to hold the two smaller pieces in place. The notches should be at least as deep as the recessed panels. So, if the panels are recessed ¾ inch below the frame of the door, the notches on either side will also be ¾ inch deep. You can make the notches with a handsaw, but a circular saw will help you save time and effort. Adjust the saw blade to the desired depth and make two parallel cuts for each notch. Then chip out the wood between the cuts with a hammer and chisel.

Fit one of the short pieces into one of the notches (the tighter the fit, the better) and nail through from the opposite side. Then, insert the other short panel into the other slot. This time, toenail (nail at an angle) the two pieces together. For added stability, nail a ¼x2-inch piece of pine lath to the top of the cross members, then two more pieces to the top edges of the long parts of the base. Top it all off with a sheet of glass that's ½ or ⅝ inch thick and slightly longer and wider than the table base.

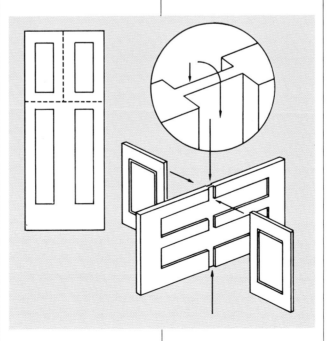

Even if you're a complete bungler when it comes to building things, rest assured you can "construct" this attractive coffee table with the greatest of ease. The secret to the table's simplicity lies in the fact that not a single nail is involved. The only building talent you need is the ability to stack pieces of wood.

Have the lumberyard cut top-grade 1x4s in an equal number of long and short pieces (the dimensions will depend on the size of table you want to make). With 1x4s in hand, simply stack and layer the pieces to the desired height. To ensure stability, dab a bit of white glue between each layer at all four corners. Top the table with a piece of ¾-inch glass that extends three inches beyond the boards on all sides. *Note:* To avoid nicking yourself, make sure to have the dealer seam the edges of the glass after it has been cut to size. For just a little more money, you can have the edges ground and polished.

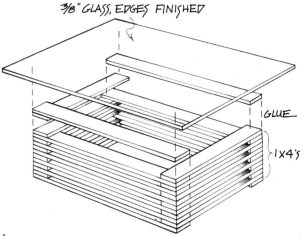

3/8" GLASS, EDGES FINISHED

GLUE

1X4'S

(GLASS TOP SHOULD EXTEND 3" BEYOND BASE ON ALL SIDES)

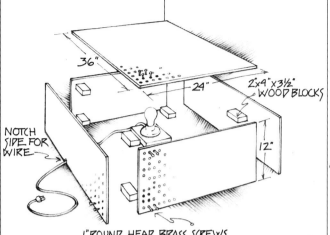

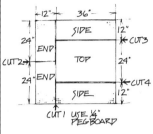

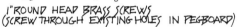

36"

24"

2"x4"x3½"
WOOD BLOCKS

12"

NOTCH
SIDE FOR
WIRE

1" ROUND HEAD BRASS SCREWS
(SCREW THROUGH EXISTING HOLES IN PEGBOARD)

12" — 36"
24" | SIDE | 12" ← CUT3
END
24" | TOP | 24"
CUT2→
24" END | SIDE | 12" ← CUT4
CUT I USE ¼"
PEGBOARD

This luminescent coffee table can be yours for the price of a large piece of perforated hardboard and a light bulb. Following the cutting pattern shown in the diagram, *far right,* cut five sections from a 48x48-inch piece of ¼-inch perforated hardboard (or, better yet, have someone at the lumberyard cut the pieces for you). To assemble the sides of the table, screw 1-inch roundhead brass screws into the corner blocks, as shown, *near right.* Once the sides are assembled, screw on the top, making sure it rests on the sides (for support).

Installing the light fixture is a mere matter of mounting a porcelain socket on a wood base, attaching a cord, and making a small notch in the perforated hardboard to facilitate running the cord to an electrical outlet.

chapter

17
Tips and Techniques

Unless you're a do-it-yourself virtuoso, there'll undoubtedly be times when you have to turn to out-side help to complete a decorating project. However, the more you can accomplish with your own two hands, the more sav-ings you're bound to realize. On the next 23 pages, you'll find countless ideas, tips, and techniques to help you do just that.

Walls and Ceilings
PAINTING POINTERS

Without question, paint is one of the most effective and least expensive decorating tools. And even if you've never painted a room before, you can easily and quickly become a "pro" simply by following the tips provided here.

Painting projects will be all the more successful if you select equipment and supplies wisely. Let your dealer advise you about primers, brushes, pads, rollers, and the kind and amount of paint to buy.

Generally, a gallon of paint will cover about 400 square feet of surface. Provide the dealer with the size of the room (the total length of all walls multiplied by the ceiling height) and the number of door and window openings. Then buy the equipment designed for the type of paint you will use.

Brushes. It is best to use a natural bristle brush with alkyds, but not with water-based paints. A latex paint will make natural bristles stick together and become mop-like. The newer disposable "brushes" that have foam instead of bristles attached to the handles are quite adequate for many projects. The small ones are useful for trim and for tiny grooves.

A high-quality paint brush will last for years if it is cleaned well after each use.

Paint rollers make quick work of coating large, flat surfaces. Make sure you have the right roller cover for your type of paint. Mohair, with its short, tightly woven nap, is best for glossy finishes; a lamb's wool cover should be used with solvent-thinned paint. Synthetic foam covers may be used with all types of paint.

Most 3-inch-wide trim rollers can reach into areas too tight for a full-size roller. Or, you may find you have more control by using a small brush to paint corners and trim areas.

Pad painters, made of a carpetlike material or foam attached to handles, spread paint easily and evenly on almost all surfaces. They're ideal for painting shakes, screens, and wide expanses of walls.

Paint trays. It's best to use a slanted (not flat), metal or plastic paint tray with grooves to help work plenty of paint into the roller cover or pad. Disposable plastic insert trays will save on cleanup time.

STEP-BY-STEP PAINTING GUIDE

1. First, prepare the walls: Fill cracks, patch plaster, scrape and sand all damaged areas, clean off dirt, and coat surfaces with the necessary primer. Then assemble your painting supplies. In addition to brushes, rollers, paint pads, and a pan, invest in plastic drop cloths and an extra roller sleeve for each color or type of paint you plan to use.

2. Fill the roller with paint by rolling it into the lower end of the tray, then smoothing it on the slanted surface until paint is distributed evenly around the roller. Fill the roller with as much paint as it will take without dripping.

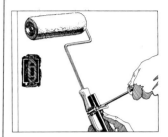

3. Paint the ceiling first, using a brush or roller attached to an extension rod (or erect a simple scaffold if you prefer). Paint in 2- or 3-foot strips across the shorter dimension of the ceiling. Use a small brush or trim roller to get into corners.

4. With a brush, edging roller, or paint pad, paint the walls by first cutting in the edges (i.e., paint a narrow strip at the ceiling line, around the doors and windows, and along the baseboards). Because lap marks won't show on flat paint, you can do all the edging around an entire room before painting the rest of the walls. With gloss paint, it's best to do one edge at a time and fill in immediately, using the roller.

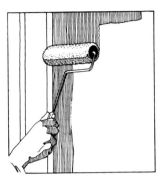

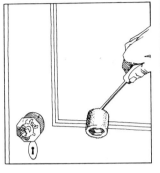

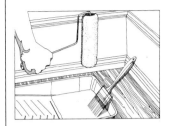

5. Switch to a roller or a paint pad for the remaining portions of the walls. If you used a brush for *edging,* run the roller close to the trim, over the brushwork, because a roller leaves a different texture than a brush does.

Some paint rollers feature guards that help prevent smearing the trim. Paint the open area of the wall first. By doing this, the roller will be dryer when you paint near the trim.

7. Painting woodwork and such features as raised door panels is time consuming, but don't rush this part of the job. If you are using the same paint for walls and woodwork, paint the woodwork as you come to it. If it will be another color or a higher gloss, do it after painting the walls. A small trim roller or an edging brush with tapered ends will make covering grooves and molding easier.

9. Windows also require time and patience. Adjust the window so you can paint the lower part of the upper sash first. Then raise the upper sash almost to the top to finish painting it. Paint the lower sash next. Continue by painting the recessed part of the window frame, then paint the frame and windowsill.

10. Paint the baseboards last, using a brush or roller. Paint the top molding and base shoe, then fill in the space. To protect the flooring or carpet from paint drips, use wide masking tape or a cardboard or plastic guard held flush against the bottom edge of the baseboard.

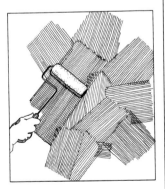

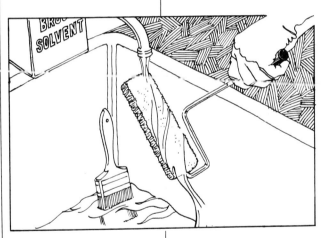

6. To paint large wall surfaces, roll a big M on the wall and then fill in. Strokes should *not* be parallel, straight up and down, or across; for best coverage, roll on paint in *every* direction.

If you're using a glossy paint, finish with vertical strokes to give the surface a smooth appearance. Use slow, smooth strokes so you won't spray tiny drops of paint. Always wipe up any spills or drops of paint immediately after they occur.

8. Paint doors in the following sequence: door frame, then the top, back, and front edges of the door itself. If the door is paneled, paint panels and molding, then the rest of the door, starting at the top.

If it's not possible to remove the door hardware, carefully paint around it with a trim brush and fill in the flat surfaces with a regular roller or a larger brush.

11. Clean-up chores include both the room and the equipment. Remove masking tape; wipe or chip off with a razor blade any drops of paint you may have missed. Clean brushes, pads, and rollers according to directions on the paint can label. Soak brushes and pads in a metal can filled with the proper thinner. Work the brush up and down to get out the paint. Use a putty knife to remove paint caked on the bristles and ferrule. Fan and squeeze the brush with your fingers to work the paint from the heel. If you intend to use the brush the following day, dry it out somewhat by rubbing it back and forth across several thicknesses of newspaper.

If you have been using a latex paint, put the pan in a tub and let water run into it slowly while you roll the roller back and forth. This cleans the pan as well as the roller. When the water in the pan begins to clear, pull the roller cover from the handle and run more water through the center and over the sides.

WALL COVERING HOW-TO

Admittedly, wallpapering a room calls for more patience and expertise than that required in painting. But there's no need to feel intimidated. The wall covering manufacturers have done a wonderful job of creating papers and other coverings that are amazingly easy to hang. Paying attention to detail is the key to a professional-looking job, so be sure to take time with each of these important stages.

MEASURING AND ESTIMATING

Wall coverings usually come in double- or triple-roll packages. A single roll should cover 30 square feet. (Most rolls actually contain 36 square feet of paper, but an allowance is needed for trimming and matching.) Widths range from 18 to 28 inches; some heavy vinyls are 54 inches wide.

Always check to see that the rolls are color matched; this should be no problem, if all rolls are from the same dye lot.

To determine how many rolls you will need, measure the distance around the room. Multiply this figure by the wall height from baseboard to ceiling line. Add up the square footage of all windows, doors, and other openings that will be left uncovered and subtract this sum from your total. To be doubly sure of your measurements, you may want to make a drawing of your walls on graph paper, with windows and other openings included. Allow extra footage for necessary waste—how much depends upon the amount you will lose when matching the paper's pattern. (Many dealers will help translate your figures into the number of double or triple rolls you need, if you provide exact room measurements.)

To be on the safe side, order an extra roll for future patches, and as a margin of error. It's better to order too many rolls than to run short

and have to wait for a second order to arrive. Most dealers will take back unopened rolls, except in cases of costly special-order papers.

Unless your wall covering is prepasted, now is the time to choose the proper adhesive. Follow the wall covering manufacturer's suggestion for the adhesive to use for your particular product.

If your walls are in need of a primer, check with the dealer as to which type will work best with the adhesive you plan to use.

PREPARING WALLS

All walls must be free of grease if the adhesive is to work properly. So begin by washing the walls, using a solution of water mixed with detergent or household ammonia. Kitchen and bath walls definitely should be washed thoroughly.

Handling old wall coverings. The old wall covering may or may not need to be removed. Vinyl coverings should always come off. If your new covering is paper, old wallpaper can stay, if it is still tight at the seams and edges, with no overlapping. However, if your new covering is vinyl, remove the old paper. A wide wall scraper and a steamer do a fast job of removing old, loose wallpaper (sketch 1).

Fabric- and paper-backed vinyls and strippable papers are removed by lifting a corner of a strip and then pulling. If the paper backing adheres to the wall, leave it as a liner for the new wall covering.

Unstrippable papers are a bit harder to remove. If the covering is impervious to water, sand the surface so water can penetrate to the adhesive. Apply water to the paper. For large areas, rent a steamer. For small areas, apply a mixture of warm water and vinegar with a brush. Proportions are $\frac{1}{2}$ cup vinegar to an average-size pail of water. Use a

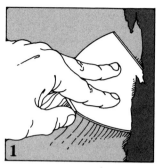

scraper to remove the paper, then remove the old paste by washing the walls with a hot water and mild soap solution.

Prepare painted walls. Wait a month before papering over any newly painted wall. For old gloss or semigloss oil-base paint, roughen with coarse sandpaper to make a good surface for the glue. Seal water-base paint with a priming coat of fast-drying glue sizing.

Unpainted walls need special treatment. Plaster should be at least a month old, and a priming coat of glue sizing should be applied.

Seal wallboard and other paper-faced surfaces with an oil-base primer (which can be very thin). Let the primer dry for at least 24 hours.

TOOLS FOR THE JOB

Tools designed specifically for wall covering are available separately or in kit form. In addition to a pasting table, ladder, drop cloth, and kraft paper, you will need the following items:
- a razor knife and several sharp new blades
- a wide (6") putty knife
- a pasting brush or roller (for prepasted wall coverings, you need a water tray and sponge instead of a pasting brush)
- a smooth brush
- a seam roller
- a yardstick
- scissors
- two plastic pails (one for paste and one for water)
- a large clean sponge
- a broad wall scraper
- a plumb bob
- a screwdriver

HANGING TIPS

You'll find that any wallpapering project will go much faster and easier if you allow plenty of work space. If you don't have a large work surface (such as sawhorses topped with a sheet of plywood or long boards), it will be worth your while to rent, borrow, or buy one.

Before tackling the rolls, make your first plumb-line mark, usually in a left corner. Snap a chalk line (sketch 2) for a true vertical where you plan to apply your first strip. (Determine the placement of the plumb line by measuring the width of the wall covering out from the corner.) Subtract ½ inch and mark your plumb line. The first strip of wall covering goes to the left of this line and is pressed into and around the corner about ½ inch (sketch 3).

Cut the first two strips after lining them up so their

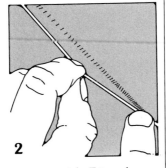

2

patterns match. Trim selvage if necessary.

Starting with the first strip, paste and "book" it by placing it on the table wrong side up and spreading paste on it from the center to the top edge of the strip. Fold the top half of the strip back to the center, pasted surfaces together. Be careful not to crease the wall covering. Repeat the procedure with the bottom half of the strip.

While this strip is resting, paste the second strip. If you cut all the strips for a wall at one time, be sure to mark one end "up" and number the strips consecutively so you won't get confused.

Hang the first booked strip by opening the top half and lining up the motif at the top. Position on the wall to the left of the plumb line, working from the center to sides without stretching the covering. Smooth the wall

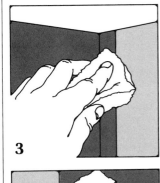

3

4

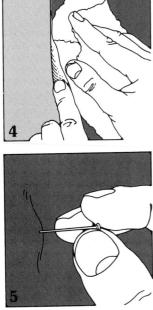

5

covering by wiping with a clean sponge or a paperhanger's brush (sketch 4).

For prepasted paper, reroll the strips, patterned side in, starting from the bottom. Then place the roll in the water box so the top of the strip

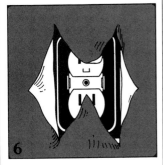

6

comes out of the box. When ready to hang the strip, place the box on the floor below where the strip will be hung. Then just draw the roll up onto the wall and smooth the covering into position along the plumb line.

Careful brushing with the wall brush will help to eliminate air pockets. If necessary, use a pin (sketch 5) to work out the wrinkles and bubbles. After you've checked the positioning, trim the strip at the top and bottom, then go on to the next strip. Line up the second strip with the first, butting it carefully to the edge of the first strip. After 15 minutes, smooth the butted edges with a seam roller. Remove the squeezed-out paste with a sponge and clean water. Flocked or raised-pattern wall coverings require a different procedure; consult the dealer for information.

Check your work periodically to see that the strips are properly aligned. Start a new plumb line on each wall and after doorways just to make sure your strips are straight. Paper around doors, windows, and other openings as you come to them.

For protruding fixtures and electrical outlets that you can't remove or disconnect, use a razor blade to cut an X in the wall covering, then slip it over the fixture (sketch 6).

UPHOLSTERED WALLS

Upholstering a wall is a bit more complicated than simply stapling fabric to the wall, but the end result is very effective. The upholstering covers up badly scarred walls, helps muffle sound within the room, and provides some sound deadening from room to room. It also gives a feeling of softness to an area.

The materials you need are a fabric with a pattern that conceals seams (such as stripes or prints), quilt batting to cover the wall in a single thickness, a sewing machine, and a staple gun.

To begin upholstering, staple the quilt batting over the entire surface of the wall. Staple batting 2 inches in from the edges at the top, bottom, sides, and around windows and doors. Place staples approximately 1 foot apart. After attaching the edges, staple randomly over the entire wall surface to anchor the batting and keep it from sagging.

Prepare the fabric by cutting strips the height of the wall from floor to ceiling, plus an extra 1½ inches at both the top and the bottom. As you cut the strips, be sure the fabric pattern matches.

Sew the strips together along the side edges with a minimum ½-inch seam. Make one large fabric piece as wide as the wall, allowing an additional 1½ inches at each side. Press the seams open on the reverse side of the fabric.

Attach the fabric to the wall by folding the top 1½ inches under the quilt batting, then stapling through both backing and fabric. Place the staples at 3-inch intervals. Then stretch fabric to the base and staple, pulling taut so no ripples occur. *Make sure the design of the fabric is vertical and straight.* Cut out inside doors and windows, leaving a hem to turn. Staple around openings. Finally, staple fabric down the sides at each end of the wall. Cover staples with trim if needed.

Windows
MEASURING AND INSTALLATION

There are no hard and fast rules when it comes to decorating windows. Such factors as size and shape of the windows, the presence or absence of a view, energy considerations, and the purposes for which the room is used should have a bearing on the kind of treatment you choose. Once you've decided on the treatment itself, the next step is to take careful measurements. Read the following guidelines to help ensure a proper fit.

Draperies and the rods you hang them on are inseparable. For this reason, you need to know the length of the rod to accurately determine the drapery width. And to establish the length of the drapery rod, you must know the size of the area you want your draperies to cover. The best way to solve this which-comes-first riddle is to follow these two rules of thumb.

For ready-made draperies, buy the width that best covers the area you want treated, then buy and install an appropriate-length rod. Take into consideration that your drapery panels will have to overlap 2 inches at the center and must cover the "returns" on each end. (Returns are the areas between the front edge of the rod and the wall or casing it's mounted on.)

For custom draperies or draperies you sew yourself, determine the exact area you want covered, buy and install the rod, then use the rod to establish the measurements of the finished draperies.

MEASURING TIPS
When measuring for draperies and drapery hardware, always use a steel tape. A cloth measuring tape may stretch somewhat, giving you inaccurate measurements.

To avoid costly mistakes, always write down all the measurements as you make them. Don't rely on your memory.

Measure every window you intend to treat, even though several windows in a room may appear to be the same size. Size is deceptive, and certain windows, particularly those in older homes, can vary slightly (but significantly) in their measurements.

INSTALLING THE ROD
Drapery hardware may be mounted in four ways: on the wall, on the casing, inside the casing, or on the ceiling. Rods to be mounted on or inside the casing can be only a certain length: the distance from outside edge to outside edge of the casing or the distance inside the window casing. Rods mounted on the wall or on the ceiling can be any length you want. The window size doesn't have to determine the size of the rod or the finished drapery.

Rods that are longer than the width of the window visually expand its size and give the window more importance than it might have on its own. Rods mounted on the wall influence the length, as well as the width, of the draperies. If desired, you can place a wall-mounted rod at the ceiling line, thus creating a floor-to-ceiling drapery effect. If not installed at ceiling height, wall-mounted rods are usually placed 4 inches above the window glass to mask the heading and hardware when the window is viewed from the outside.

The length of the rod establishes how much of the window will be exposed. If you're not using an extra-wide drapery for a special decorating effect, you will want to compute just how wide your draperies have to be to pull open and yet reveal the entire glass area of the window. This means allowing extra space at either side of the window for the draperies to "stack" when opened. This "stackback" can add up to nearly one-half the width of the glass.

To help calculate the total amount of stackback for each window, simply divide the window's glass width by three, then add 12 inches to this measurement. This will give you the total stacking area required for a pair of draperies. To determine the correct position of your rod, divide the stackback figure in half, measure that distance from either outside edge of the glass, and make a mark. The distance between these marks represents the rod length you will need.

When planning for decorative traverse or café curtain rods, take into consideration that the measurement of the rod does not include the end pieces or finials. If space is tight or if you're working on a corner installation, be sure to figure the size of the end pieces or finials into your window treatment.

MEASURING FOR DRAPERIES
Once the rods are installed, you're ready to measure for custom-made draperies.

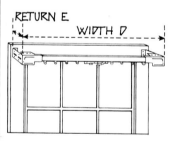

Start by carefully measuring the length of the rod from bracket to bracket. Then add 4 inches for overlap at the center of the window plus the measurement of the returns (see sketch, *above*). The sum of these three measurements will give you the finished width of your draperies.

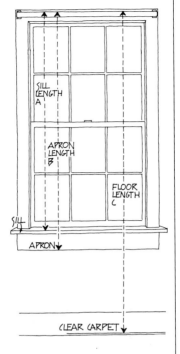

To establish the best length for finished draperies, follow these helpful tips:

To find the length of draperies or curtains hung by hooks from conventional traverse rods or curtain rods, simply measure from the top of the installed rod. If you're planning to use decorative traverse rods or café rods with rings, measure from the bottom of the rings.

Personal taste and the type of installation dictate where the hem of the draperies should be. The usual lengths are from the top of the rod (or the bottom of the rings) to the sill, apron, or floor (see sketch, *above*).

Draperies and curtains hung from wall-mounted rods usually look best if they fall to the bottom of the window's apron or to the floor. Full-length curtains and draperies should barely clear the floor or carpet. For rooms with baseboard heating, be sure to choose a style and length that will not interfere with the airflow of the heating unit.

Draperies and curtains hanging from rods installed on the casing most frequently fall to the windowsill or to the bottom of the apron. Curtains hung from inside-the-casing-mounted rods should drop only to the sill.

DOUBLE-CHECK MEASUREMENTS

The importance of double-checking all drapery measurements can't be stressed enough. Here's a summary of the basics for measuring the width of standard draperies, plus several other popular window treatments:

Draw draperies: Measure the length of the rod, plus the returns and overlap at the center. Remember that one-way draw traverse rods have no overlap.

Café curtains: Measure the width of the rods between the finials. To determine the length of each tier, measure from the lower part of the clip or ring on the upper rod to about 3 inches below the clip or ring on the lower rod. This is the finished length (including overlap).

If you're using decorative café rods, you may want the bottom rods and rings exposed rather than hidden. If so, measure from the bottom of the ring on the top rod to the top of the lower rod.

For the lower tier, measure from the bottom of the ring on the lower rod to the desired finished length (to the sill, the apron, or the floor).

Recessed window curtains (mounted inside the casing): Measure the length from the top of the rod to the sill.

Shirred curtains: Finished length is from 1 inch above the top of the rod (this allows a 1-inch heading above the rod pocket) to the desired length (the sill, apron, or floor).

INSTALLATION IS IMPORTANT

Measuring accurately, installing the right rod in the right place, and selecting quality draperies all contribute to a nicely finished, professional-looking window treatment. But all of these preliminaries are a waste of time unless the curtains or draperies are properly installed.

Hooks play a big part in how well a drapery panel hangs. Several types are available; look for the one that's right for your particular drapery and rod combination. If in doubt, ask a salesperson in the drapery section of a department store, or check the rod package for suggestions.

Remember that hook placement determines the placement of the drapery or curtain heading in relationship to the rod. Learn where the heading should be for each type of rod, then place the hooks appropriately.

For conventional traverse rod installations (or for curtain rods), the heading top should be level with the rod top. This conceals the rod when the window treatment is closed.

With decorative traverse rods or café curtain rods, you'll want the rod and rings to show, so the top of the heading should come to the bottom of the rings.

A properly installed drapery or curtain covers the entire casing of the window. Pleats should be straight and the space between pleats should be smooth and even when the draperies are closed. The same smooth, sleek look should be evident in the return area from the outside front edge of the rod to the wall surface. Overlaps should be smooth and the two drapery panels should line up evenly at the center when draperies are closed.

GETTING THE HANG OF IT

The way you hang your draperies can also make a big difference in the way they operate on a traverse rod.

Start by hanging the panels at the master slide in the center of the rod. Then attach a drapery hook in each slide, working toward the end of the rod. Don't skip rings or slides if there are more than you need. Extra slides may interfere with the operation of the traverse rod. Instead, push extra slides to the end of the rod and slip them out of the unit.

If draperies are to have a professional look when they're opened, the headings must be trained to fold up neatly. To train draperies hung from a conventional traverse rod, place your finger behind the drapery heading in the center of the space between two pleats. Bring your finger forward and hand-press the drapery heading, creasing in the center of the space. Continue this procedure across the entire heading of the drapery. Creasing drapery headings in this fashion lets you determine where the headings will fold when opened, and also helps control the symmetry and neatness of the window treatment.

To train the headings of draperies hung from decorative traverse rods, use the same procedure, but rather than crease the heading forward, away from the window, crease it backward, toward the window. In this case, the drapery hangs below the rod so there is space for excess folds of fabric to recede, creating a trim silhouette.

The next step in "breaking in" your draperies is to train the folds in each panel. To form attractive, professional-looking folds, open up the draperies and finger-press each fold. Using tape, heavy twine or a strip of fabric, tie the folds loosely in position. The panels should stay tied for two or three days to train the fabric into the even folds you want. Wrinkles will hang out after you've untied the draperies.

DRAPERY CARE

Draperies will last longer and look better if you have them dry-cleaned or laundered on a regular basis. (Not all fabrics can stand up to laundering, so be sure to check the fiber content. If in doubt, dry cleaning is recommended.) Also, for best results, be sure to tell the cleaner the fiber content of the draperies.

DRAPERY SHOPPING

Although you don't have to buy new draperies or curtains (or replace old ones) very often, when the time comes, watch out: the expense can be considerable. As is usually the case with any major household expenditure, your best defense against high costs is to arm yourself with as much product information as possible.

Drapery decisions are best made at home, not in a store. That's because the type of light (both natural and artificial) and the areas of surrounding color and pattern have a great visual effect on a window treatment. If at all possible, take drapery samples home on approval (or buy ¼ to ½ yard of drapery fabric) before making any purchase decisions. Hang or tape the sample at a window in the room where the new draperies will be hung. Only by doing this can you get an accurate idea if the color, pattern, texture, and "weight" are right for the window (and decor) in question. If for some reason it's not possible to bring samples home, then take swatches of your carpet, upholstery, and other color samples to the store when making preliminary selections.

FABRIC FUNDAMENTALS

The *kind* of fabric you select for your draperies is just as important as color and style considerations. Some of the most important qualities in a window treatment, such as durability and easy care, are directly influenced by the fiber, the dyes, the weave, and the finish applied to the fabric. All of these factors work together in creating a window treatment that will live up to your expectations.

Fibers, for instance, are of two kinds, natural and synthetic. Cotton, wool, silk, and linen are all natural fibers. Three of the naturals—cotton, linen, and wool—are quite durable. Silk, though exquisite, is more fragile and not used in draperies.

Synthetics used for drapery fabrics include acetate, acrylic, nylon, polyester, rayon, and glass fibers. You can choose from several brand names by different manufacturers in each fabric category.

Acetate is noted for its soft touch, good draping qualities, quick-drying properties, excellent crease retention, and sun, moth, and mildew resistance.

Acrylic is best known for its soft, wool-like feel, and its resistance to wrinkles, moths, mildew, and fire. Some acrylic fabrics are washable; others must be dry-cleaned.

Nylon fabrics are strong and pleat well. They can be washed or dry-cleaned, are wrinkle resistant, and will not sag or stretch. Bright-color yarns are more sun resistant than the duller yarns.

Polyester fabrics or blends of polyester and other fibers are popular because of their easy-care properties. These fabrics are durable, drip-drying, and wrinkle resistant, as well as high in sun resistance and crease retention.

Rayon is often blended with other fibers. Basically, it is soft, inexpensive, wrinkle and abrasion resistant, and drapes well. There are numerous rayon blends, so be sure to read the hangtags carefully.

Glass fiber is remarkably easy to care for. Fabrics of these fibers drape well, need no ironing, and dry rapidly. They are excellent resisters of sun, mildew, moths, and fire.

Some fabrics are blends of both natural and synthetic fibers and are designed to bring out the best qualities of each fiber.

When shopping for draperies, always look for fiber content labels that explain the fabric's characteristics and care requirements. Be sure to file these labels for future reference so you can maintain the fabrics correctly.

Fabric weaves can be plain, twill, satin, knit, or a variation of these. Remember that the more closely woven a fabric is, the greater its durability and stretch resistance are likely to be.

Fabric finishes give draperies their special characteristics. Finishes are available to provide easier care; to add body, luster, and crispness to the fabric; to make fabrics moth-, water-, and shrink-proof; to make them mildew, bacteria, and flame resistant; to provide wrinkle and crease resistance; and to make them stain and soil repellent.

Read labels on your draperies or drapery fabric to find out what finishes have been applied, what they do, and how long they will last. If finishes aren't permanent, find out whether the fabric can be refinished and what the cost will be.

DRAPERY OPTIONS

If you decide to buy your draperies or have them made (as opposed to sewing them yourself), the options are many and varied.

Among your choices are ready-made draperies, special-order and mail-order ready-mades, made-to-measure draperies (or factory-made customs); workroom customs; and draperies selected through a department store's in-home shopping service. The in-home service gives you factory-made customs, but with some design options usually found only in workroom custom-made draperies. If you're not familiar with all these terms, read on.

• *Ready-mades* are convenient if you're short on time, money, or both. They're available in a variety of fabrics, colors, and patterns and are the least expensive of your choices. Generally, you can expect to pay about half the price of workroom customs and 40 to 60 percent less than factory-made custom draperies. Aside from cost, the main advantage of ready-mades is their immediacy; no waiting is involved. You simply walk into the store, make your purchase, take the ready-mades home, and hang them. Ready-mades do have a drawback, however: They're available in standard sizes only. So if your window is irregularly shaped, sized, or positioned, you may be out of luck.

Finding ready-made draperies in the width you want is generally less of a problem than finding the right length. Standard sizes are 63 inches long by 48, 72, or 96 inches wide per pair, and 84 inches long by 48, 72, 96, 122, or 144 inches wide per pair. Ready-mades are available in unlined, thermal-lined, and fabric-lined versions, but you may have to shop around to find the kind you want.

• *Made-to-measure draperies* are sometimes referred to as special-order ready-mades or as factory-made customs. Translated, each label means the same. Here's how it works: You choose the fabric from store samples and provide accurate window measurements, then draperies are made to your specifications (up to 108 inches in length).

Prices in this category of window covering vary greatly. The differences are generally due to the fullness of the drapery and the quality of the workmanship.

You can expect made-to-measure draperies to arrive in four to eight weeks.

• *Workroom customs* are draperies made in the workroom of either a retail store or a decorator shop. They're the high end of the drapery buying spectrum and offer the advantages of unlimited selection of fabrics, styles, and sizes. The price includes delivery to your home. Installation of the rods and draperies themselves may or may not be included in the price.

Workroom customs usually call for a professional measurement at the start to prevent any mistake in width and length. The measuring service generally is considered part of the job and comes at no extra charge to you. Charges for workroom customs depend on the price of the fabric, whether the draperies are lined or unlined, the labor charge, and the price of the hooks. This type of drapery will cost you about twice what ready-mades of a similar fabric would cost, providing you could get them in the style and size you wanted. Workroom customs take from four to eight weeks for delivery, depending on the availability and arrival of the fabrics ordered.

• *Shop-at-home draperies.* Many large department stores offer the convenient service of shopping for draperies (and other window treatments, including blinds, shades, and shutters) at home. Here's how the service works: A representative of the store comes to your home with numerous fabric samples and window treatment ideas in hand. (The representative is usually a knowledgeable professional, but not necessarily an interior designer.) After you've selected the fabric and any new drapery hardware needed, the representative takes measurements of the windows and gives you a cost estimate based on the price of the fabric and the style of treatment you've chosen. The cost of these draperies usually is less than workroom custom draperies, but more than made-to-measures. The savings comes from the difference in volume of business and labor costs of large versus small custom drapery shops.

Here again, the waiting time for shop-at-home draperies is approximately six to eight weeks.

• *Mail-order* companies offer still another way to shop for draperies and other window treatments without leaving home. The catalogs feature numerous styles to choose from in either illustration or photograph form. You decide on the treatment you want, then place your order by mail or phone. Most drapery treatments are designed for standard-size windows, and only the large, store-connected companies can accommodate custom or special orders. Prices vary, but generally you can expect to get good value and attractive styling at very reasonable prices.

LINED OR UNLINED?

If you're hanging anything other than sheers or casements, a lining fabric should be considered. While they aren't essential, drapery linings are worth having for a number of practical and aesthetic reasons.

Among their advantages, linings help draperies hang more smoothly with deeper, richer-looking folds. They protect carpet and upholstery fabrics, as well as the fabric of the draperies themselves, from bright sunlight and fading. And, in these days of concern for energy conservation, a drapery lining is one of the easiest and most effective ways to reduce heat loss through the glass during winter months and stop infiltration of heat in the summer. Extra energy savings can be realized by using a thermal lining. (For more information about energy savings, see page 118.)

There's one more advantage to incorporating linings with drapery treatment—an advantage that's easy to overlook if you're viewing the draperies only from inside your home. Draperies are also seen from the outside, and linings will give a uniform appearance to your house exterior.

WHY QUALITY PAYS OFF

The better the quality of the draperies you buy, whether they're ready-mades or customs, the more satisfied you're likely to be. True, you'll have to pay a premium for good-quality drapery fabric and workmanship, but both elements are definitely worth the increase in price.

Here are some of the points to check when shopping for draperies:

Good construction is essential to the durability and appearance of draperies. Look for straight hems and square corners—both are indications of good-quality construction. If hems and corners are anything but straight, the drapery will never hang well. Stitching, too, should be neat and straight.

Pattern matching is yet another key to the quality of workmanship. If the fabric you've chosen has a design, make sure that the patterns match perfectly, not only in the seams within each panel, but also from one panel to the other when hung at the window.

You may have an opportunity to choose how full you want your draperies, consequently determining how deep the pleats will be. Full draperies with deep pleats cost more but hang better and look better—and only a high-quality workshop will offer you that choice.

Deal only with a reputable outlet, whether it is a local store, a national department store, or a private decorator shop. Ask to see draperies made by the firm with which you are dealing and judge the quality of the workmanship before you decide to place your order.

HOW TO SEW DRAPERIES

Home sewing means big savings when it comes to fabric window treatments. And, making your own draperies is not as difficult as you might think. Perseverance, patience, and an ability to work carefully are the main talents you need to complete a successful drapery sewing project.

MEASURE FIRST

Meticulous measurements are a must for any do-it-yourself drapery treatment. Always use a steel tape or wood ruler to obtain accurate measurements. Start by measuring the area the draperies will cover. To this finished-length measurement, add 11 inches for hems on unlined draperies (6 inches for the bottom hem, 5 inches for the heading covering the stiffening material). Add 7 inches to the finished length for lined draperies (6 inches for the bottom hem and 1 inch at the top).

If the fabric has a design repeat, determine how many inches apart the repeat is and divide that figure into the length measurement of your panel. If the result is a fraction, buy enough extra yardage for one more full pattern repeat per width. Plan for a full pattern motif at the heading of floor-length draperies, and, if necessary, a portion of the design at the hem.

To establish the width of your drapery panel, measure the rod from bracket to bracket. Double the measurement (or triple it for extra fullness), add the space of the returns plus 4 inches for overlap at the center of the two panels and 8 inches for side hems. This sum, divided by the width of the fabric you've chosen, will tell you just how many widths of fabric each panel will require. Add 1 extra inch in width for every seam where two cuts of fabric are joined. Divide this final figure in half to determine the unfinished width of each drapery panel.

You can determine the finished width of your drapery panels by using pleating tape until you reach the desired finished width. Remove the pins, measure the tape, and add appropriate inches for the seams and hems.

CUT WITH CARE

Lay the fabric on a flat surface. Always be sure to cut with the true crosswise grain, established by pulling a thread in the fabric, then cutting along the thread line.

Cut away the selvages or clip them to prevent puckering seams. Cut a master fabric panel, then lay it on the remaining fabric and cut all other panels.

If lining draperies, cut the lining fabric 6 inches shorter and 3 inches narrower than the face fabric.

ONE STEP AT A TIME

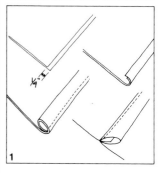

Carefully complete each step of the sewing process, finishing the same step on all panels before proceeding to the next step.

First, sew fabric cuts together, using an interlocking fell seam (sketch 1).

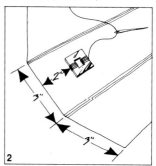

Next, finish the hem, whether you're sewing lined or unlined draperies. Turn up 3 inches of the drapery fabric and press in place. Turn this pressed hem a second time and press (sketch 2). Position weights according to the sketch and tack in place. Hand-hem or machine-stitch the bottom hem.

To hem the lining, turn under 1 inch and press. Turn the hem a second time. Press and stitch.

LINED OR UNLINED?

If you're sewing unlined draperies, your next steps are the placement of the stiffening to create the heading, then the side hems. If sewing lined draperies, reverse the procedure and sew the side hems, then the heading.

For unlined draperies, cut a piece of stiffening material 4 inches shorter than the width of the drapery panel. Place the material on the wrong side of the fabric, 1 inch down from the top edge and 2 inches in from each side edge. Fold the 1 inch of fabric down onto the stiffening and stitch along the top folded edge. Then turn the entire stiffening material over toward the wrong side of the fabric and stitch down.

Next, sew the side seams, turning 1 inch under and pressing down. Repeat, turning the hem a second time. Press and stitch. Miter corners where side hems and bottom hem meet.

For lined draperies, lay the lining fabric on top of the drapery fabric, right sides together, with the tops of both the lining and the drapery fabrics even. Pin the edges of one side of the two fabrics together and stitch ½ inch in from the cut edge (sketch 3). Place the two other side edges together and sew with ½-inch seam allowance. (Remember, drapery fabric is wider than lining fabric so the two will not lie flat.)

After sewing the side seams, turn the panel right

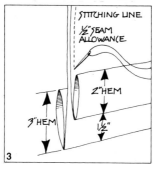

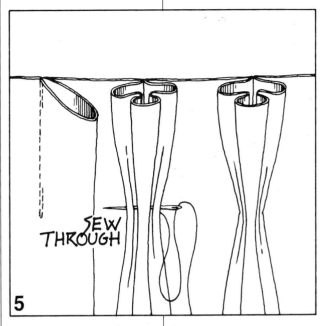

5 SEW THROUGH

side out and press down, positioning lining 1½ inches in from the folded edge of drapery panel. Press. Miter corners where side seams meet the hem.

To create a heading of buckram or crinoline, cut stiffening material the width of the finished, pressed panel. Turn the panel the wrong side out again and place the buckram at the top edge of the panel with the bottom edge of the stiffening material ½ inch below the top edge of the drapery panel. Stitch down, then turn the panel right side out. The stiffening is hidden between the drapery fabric and lining. Press down and pleat.

If using pleater tape, place drapery fabric right side up and lay pleater tape on the top edge with pocket openings facing up. The tape should overlap the drapery fabric ½ inch and extend ½ inch at each side. Make sure end pockets are equidistant from the ends of the panel.

Sew the tape ¼ inch from the edge. Turn the drapery over and fold back the tape so it lies against the lining fabric. Allow ½-inch margin between the top of the pleater tape and the top fold of the drapery panel. Press.

To give pleater tape a finished appearance, fold under the overhanging ½ inch of tape on each side and sew it to the drapery lining edge. Stitch along the bottom edge of the pleater tape, below the pockets.

PERFECT PLEATING

Because windows and draperies vary in size, there's no set rule for the spacing or the depth of pleats. The most common spacing of pleats is 4 inches apart but you may prefer to place them more closely together. There is, however, a guide for pleating draperies that can be used no matter what spacing you select. To help you with this formula, we've included an example for each step-by-step procedure.

First, determine your finished, pleated panel width, including returns and center overlap. (Let's assume that measurement is 36 inches.) Then subtract the space for the return. (A conventional traverse rod is usually 3½ or 4 inches from the wall. For the purpose of this example, subtract 4 inches from 36, leaving 32 inches.)

If you've decided to space your pleats 4 inches apart, divide this figure (32 inches) by 4 to find out the number of spaces between pleats on your drapery panel (32 divided by 4 equals 8 spaces).

Next, subtract the space of the returns from the *unpleated* width of the panel. (Let's say that the result is 60 inches.) Divide this figure (60) by the number of spaces (8). The result is 7½. Subtract the 4-inch-between-pleats space from this figure (7½) to establish the amount of fabric in each pleat (3½ inches).

Start pleating by measuring 4 inches (or the space required for the return) from the outer edge of the panel. Mark with a pin. Continue marking pleated areas and spaces, according to the formula given above, until you have the entire width of the unpleated panel marked for pleating. Be sure you finish with a 4-inch space at the

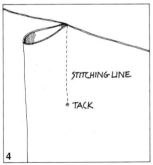

4 STITCHING LINE · TACK

center edge. This will accommodate the overlap at the center of the drapery.

To form a pleat, fold through the center of the

space marked for the pleat and pin it down. On the right side of the fabric, stitch from the top to the bottom of the stiffening material (sketch 4). Backstitch or tack to reinforce the pleat. With the basic pleat formed, you can use any of the following variations of decorative pleats.

Pinch pleats (sketch 5) are formed by dividing the large pleat into three smaller ones

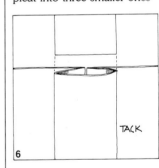

6 TACK

and stitching at the lower edge of the pleat.

French pleats (sketch 6) are like pinch pleats, but are not creased. Divide the basic pleat into 3 smaller pleats; sew through bottom of pleat.

Box pleats (sketch 7) are easily formed by pressing down the basic pleat and tacking at both the top and the bottom edges.

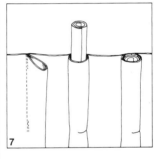

7

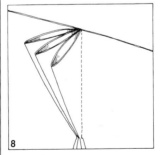

8

Cartridge pleats (sketch 8) are box pleats, but are untacked and have cotton or rolls of buckram inserted to give them their shape.

Furniture
COMMON CONSTRUCTION MATERIALS

Are you thinking of trying your hand at a do-it-yourself furniture project? If so, remember that the materials you choose will depend on the project's intended use. When making your selections, ask yourself these questions: Are you constructing something for indoor or outdoor use? Is the item intended for decorative purposes or is it strictly utilitarian in nature? Will it have light-duty use or be subjected to considerable wear and tear?

HARDBOARD

Standard hardboard is an excellent choice for cabinet-work, drawer bottoms, and concealed panels. It is available in 4x8-foot sheets and comes in ⅛- and ¼-inch thicknesses. Perforated hardboard, with holes spaced about one inch apart, is recommended for ventilated storage units and for the backs of stereo cabinets. The ¼- and ⅛-inch perforated hardboard is also great for storing garden equipment and other tools—its holes accept hooks designed for this purpose. To expand or change the arrangement, just switch the hooks around. If your planned project will be subject to dampness, use tempered hardboard.

Particleboard, chipboard, and flakeboard—also members of the hardboard family —have a coarser, grainy surface, are lighter in color, and are available in thicknesses up to ¾ inch. These products are made of granulated or shredded wood particles forced together under pressure with a binder at high temperature.

PLYWOOD

Plywood comes in 4x8-foot sheets, although larger sheets are available on special order. Thicknesses range from ⅛ inch to ¾ inch. For light-duty storage, the ¼- and ½-inch thicknesses are adequate. If you are planning to build an outdoor storage unit, specify *exterior grade* when making your purchase. Exterior grade plywood has its layers glued together with a waterproof glue to withstand rain.

The surfaces of plywood sheets are graded A, B, C, and D—A being the best, smoothest surface, and D being the least desirable in appearance. Choose AA (top grade, both sides) only for projects where both sides will be exposed; use a less expensive combination for projects where looks aren't a factor.

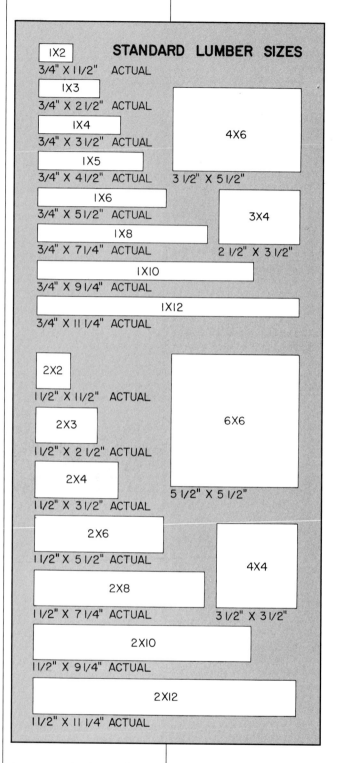

STANDARD LUMBER SIZES

IX2 — 3/4" X 1 1/2" ACTUAL
IX3 — 3/4" X 2 1/2" ACTUAL
IX4 — 3/4" X 3 1/2" ACTUAL
IX5 — 3/4" X 4 1/2" ACTUAL
IX6 — 3/4" X 5 1/2" ACTUAL
IX8 — 3/4" X 7 1/4" ACTUAL
IXIO — 3/4" X 9 1/4" ACTUAL
IXI2 — 3/4" X 11 1/4" ACTUAL

2X2 — 1 1/2" X 1 1/2" ACTUAL
2X3 — 1 1/2" X 2 1/2" ACTUAL
2X4 — 1 1/2" X 3 1/2" ACTUAL
2X6 — 1 1/2" X 5 1/2" ACTUAL
2X8 — 1 1/2" X 7 1/4" ACTUAL
2XIO — 1 1/2" X 9 1/4" ACTUAL
2XI2 — 1 1/2" X 11 1/4" ACTUAL

4X6 — 3 1/2" X 5 1/2"
3X4 — 2 1/2" X 3 1/2"
6X6 — 5 1/2" X 5 1/2"
4X4 — 3 1/2" X 3 1/2"

SOLID WOOD

Ordinary wood still ranks as the most popular building material. Wood is sold by the "board foot" (1x12x12 inches). One board foot equals the surface area of one square foot, with a nominal thickness of one inch.

Wood is marketed by "grade." For most building projects, No. 2 grade will satisfy your needs. This grade may have some blemishes, such as loose knots, but these don't reduce the strength of the wood.

If you're planning to build a unit that will be a primary factor in a room's decor, buy *select lumber*—a grade that's relatively free of blemishes and other imperfections.

Remember, too, that most outdoor projects demand highly durable grades of wood; redwood or cedar is preferable. You can use a softwood as long as you treat it for moisture resistance.

You can buy boards up to 16 feet in length and 12 inches in width, although a lumberyard may occasionally have somewhat wider or longer boards available.

Wood is divided into two categories, softwood and hardwood. Softwoods come from trees that don't shed their leaves in winter: hemlock, fir, pine, spruce, and similar evergreen cone-bearing trees. Hardwoods come from trees that do shed their leaves: maple, oak, birch, mahogany, walnut, and other broad-leaved varieties.

Wood is sold as dimension lumber or millwork lumber. Dimension is used for general construction; millwork is used in some furniture building and special items.

Also keep in mind that lumber is sold by *nominal* size. A 2x4, for example, actually measures 1½x3½ inches, and a piece of 5-quarter (5/4) material is less than 1¼ inches thick after milling. The chart, *opposite page,* shows nominal and actual sizes of most common pieces of dimension lumber. Ask lumberyard personnel for help with millwork lumber.

HARDWARE

For any type of fastening work, you will need nails, screws, and bolts, as well as glues and cements.

Nails are sold by the penny, which has nothing to do with their cost. The "penny" (abbreviated *d*) refers to the size. Use common nails for general-purpose work, finishing and casing nails for trim or cabinetwork, and brads for attaching molding to walls and furniture.

Screws are sold by length and diameter. The diameter is indicated by a number, from 1 to 16. The thicker the screw shank, the larger the number. Always drill a pilot hole when inserting a screw into hardwood, and always drill a clearance hole in the leading piece of wood when screwing two pieces of wood together. Without a clearance hole, the leading piece tends to "hang up," preventing a tight fit between the two.

Some of the most common screws include flathead, roundhead, and ovalhead wood screws. These are used for the great majority of building projects where fastening wood to wood and other joints is required. Use hanger and lag screws to make joints that can be dismantled without using a bolt. Use thread formers in thicker metals and in plywood applications. Dowel screws are good choices for end joints where one piece of wood can turn. Self-tapping screws come in two varieties—solid and split—and are used for thin sheet metal applications.

Bolts also can be used to fasten wood together, but only if there is access to the back for the required washer and nut. A bolted joint is stronger than a screwed joint, because the bolt diameter is generally thicker than the comparable screw, and the wrench used to tighten the nut can apply much more force than a screwdriver in a screw slot.

Like screws, bolts come in many varieties for different fastening purposes. Machine bolts are designed for all-around heavy-duty applications. Carriage bolts are handy for joining 2-inch and thicker boards. Use stove bolts for normal-duty situations, expansion bolts for heavy-duty applications on masonry walls, and toggle bolts for hollow wall situations. Flange bolts also can be used for hollow walls, but they're difficult to remove.

GLUES AND CEMENTS

Though not "hardware" as such, glues and cements are important tools for any fastening job.

White glue is excellent for use with wood, paper, and cloth, and only moderate clamping pressure is required. No mixing is involved, and the glue dries crystal clear. However, white glue is not waterproof, so don't use it for work that is subjected to excessive dampness, or for outdoor projects.

Epoxy glue. Use the two-tube epoxy glue for joints that must be waterproof.

Plastic resin glue, a powder that you mix with water for a creamy consistency, is highly water-resistant and works well as a wood-to-wood adhesive.

Contact cement is waterproof and provides an excellent bond between wood and wood, and between wood and plastic. When working with contact cement, remember that it dries instantly; you must position your surfaces together exactly as you want them, because you won't get a second chance.

True waterproof glue comes in two containers; one holds a liquid resin, the other a powder catalyst. When dry, this type of glue is absolutely waterproof and can be safely used for garden equipment and all outdoor projects and furniture.

MISCELLANEOUS HARDWARE

There are many types of hardware accessories that come in handy when you're constructing storage bins, cabinets, chests, shelves, and other building projects.

Here are some accessories you may need from time to time: Corrugated fasteners connect two boards or mend splits in wood; angle irons reinforce corners; flat and T plates also reinforce work; masonry nails secure work to concrete or brick walls; steel plates with a threaded center are used for attaching legs to cabinets; screw eyes and cup hooks are useful for hanging items inside storage units; and lag screw plugs made of lead or plastic secure furring strips or shelf brackets to masonry walls.

BASIC JOINERY TECHNIQUES

The more you know about basic joinery techniques, the more masterful you'll be as a do-it-yourselfer. To help you get started, we've provided a brief overview of some of the more common joints you're likely to come across. Real knowledge of joinery techniques, however, comes from "hands-on" experience. So if you're a novice, it would be well worth your while to take a beginner's woodworking course.

BUTT JOINTS

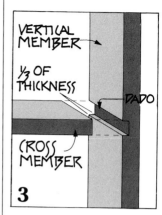

Of all wood joinery techniques, the butt joint is the easiest to make, but it's also one of the weakest. A butt joint consists of two pieces of wood meeting at a right angle and held together with nails or screws (sketch 1). Adding a dab of glue before using the nails or screws will make the joint more secure.

DADO JOINTS

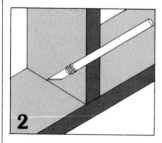

Used mainly to anchor bookcase shelves, cabinet shelves, stair treads, and drawer components, a dado joint is simply a recessed cut through the face or edge of a piece of lumber. The dado's popularity stems from its strength and good looks. To make a dado joint, draw two parallel lines with a knife across the face of the work equal to the thickness of the wood it is to engage (sketch 2). The depth should be about one-third of the thickness of the wood (sketch 3).

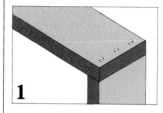

VERTICAL MEMBER

⅓ OF THICKNESS

DADO

CROSS MEMBER

Next, use a backsaw to make cuts on these lines and one or more cuts between the lines, then chisel away the remaining wood.

You can speed up the job by using a router, or a circular, table, or radial arm saw. Any one of these power tools makes the cutting of dadoes an easy job, and provides greater accuracy than can be achieved by hand.

If appearance is a factor, consider the stopped dado joint. With this type of joint, the dado (the cutaway part) extends only partway, and only a portion of the shelf is cut away to match the non-cut part of the dado.

To make a stopped dado, first make your guide marks and chisel away a small area at the stopped end to allow for saw movement (sketch 4).

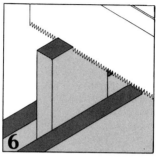

Then make saw cuts along your guide marks to the proper depth. Next, chisel out the wasted wood as shown (sketch 5). Finally, cut away a corner of the connecting board to accommodate the stopped dado (sketch 6).

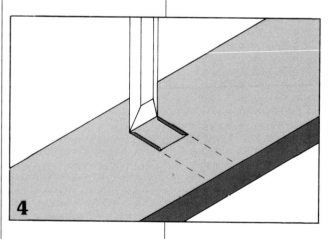

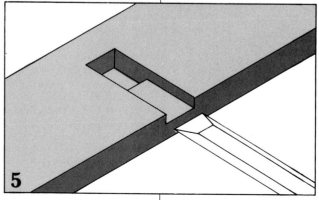

RABBET JOINTS

The rabbet joint is really a partial dado. As indicated in the drawing (sketch 7), only one of the meeting members is cut away.

The rabbet joint is simple to construct and is quite strong. You can ensure an extra measure of strength by securing the meeting members with nails or with screws and glue.

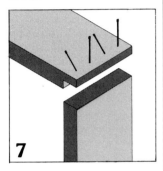

This joint is frequently used in the construction of inset backs for units such as cabinets and bookshelves (sketch 8). To make this joint, rabbet each of the framing members, then carefully measure the distance between the rabbeted openings. Cut the back accordingly.

Although it's possible to secure rabbet joints by using only adhesive, you'll get a much better joint if you also use screws or nails.

Sometimes, screws with decorative washers can enhance the appearance of a project, especially if the joint is being used for bookcases, shelf units, or open-shelf hutch cabinets.

If possible, clamp rabbet joints until the adhesive sets. If you can't clamp the joint, choose a fast-setting adhesive. Be sure not to overfill the joints with adhesive.

For additional strength, you can combine dado and rabbeting techniques in certain projects, such as drawer construction.

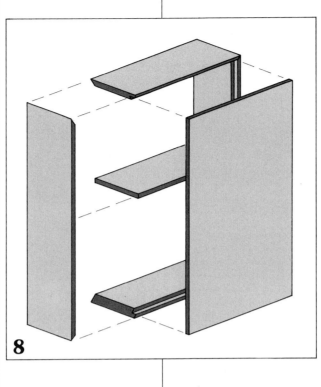

MITER JOINTS

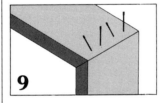

For clean good looks, few joinery techniques can outdo the miter. It is used primarily for projects that require a touch of elegance—corners of cabinet bases, casings, and picture frame moldings. In simple terms, a miter consists of two pieces of wood meeting at a right angle.

Though they're fairly easy to make, miters do have one liability—they're somewhat weak. To make them stronger, it is usually necessary to reinforce the joint with metal angles, gussets, or mending plates. If you fear that these add-ons will detract from the appearance of the project, splines or dowels can more discreetly strengthen the joint.

To make a miter joint, you'll need a miter box and a backsaw or power saw that you can adjust to cut at a 45-degree angle. Unless you plan to do a great deal of mitering, purchase an inexpensive miter box.

The simple miter joint is a surface joint with no shoulders for support, so you must reinforce it. The easiest way to do this is with nails and

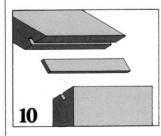

glue (sketch 9). Most picture frames are made this way, but for cabinet and furniture work, you may use other means of reinforcement. One method is to use a hardwood spline as shown (sketch 10). Apply glue to the spline and to the mitered area and clamp as shown (sketch 11) until the glue dries.

A variation of the long spline uses several short splines (at least three) that are inserted at opposing angles.

Dowels also are a popular method of reinforcing mitered

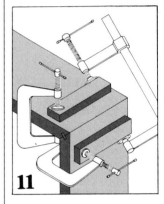

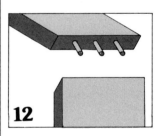

joints (sketch 12). Careful drilling of the holes is necessary to make certain the dowel holes align.

Use dowels that are slightly shorter than the holes they are to enter to allow for glue at the bottom. Score or roughen the dowels so the glue will adhere better for a strong bond.

RENEWING OLD FURNITURE

Rejuvenating old furniture offers many rewards, not the least of which is saving money. So if you own (or happen to come across) a timeworn or damaged sofa, chair, or some other furniture piece, think twice before you pass it by. The piece might be worth saving—for both practical and decorative purposes.

HOW TO REFINISH OLD FURNITURE

Refinishing can make wood furniture look better than new. However, before you embark on a complete refinishing job, first determine whether an all-out effort is really necessary. It could be that all the piece needs is a thorough cleaning. To determine whether cleaning is all that's needed, wash a good-size section of the piece with paint thinner. If a white haze appears, buff it away with extra-fine steel wool. Then apply several coats of wax. If the results are satisfactory, refinishing is not necessary and you'll have saved yourself a lot of time and work.

Next, take a good look at the grain of the wood and at the overall condition of the piece. Clear, natural finishes are meant to bring out the beauty of wood. If the wood isn't attractive, the piece may not be worth refinishing.

REMOVING OLD FINISH

Unless you decide to take your piece to a professional furniture stripper, your first step in the refinishing process is to remove all the old finish. Paint or varnish remover will soften paint, varnish, and almost any other brush-on finish so you can lift it off with a scraper or a spray of water, depending on the type of remover you use. There are many removers available today, but they fall into three basic categories: paste, semi-paste, and liquid. All will remove the old finish, but for indoor use, a nonflammable, nontoxic paste is best.

Whichever type of remover you choose, you should always take some general commonsense precautions:
• Wear rubber gloves to protect your hands. If your hands perspire in rubber gloves, wear cotton gloves inside the rubber ones.
• Always work in a well-ventilated room (or outdoors, if possible) and take frequent fresh-air breaks.
• Stripping off old finish is a messy job, so cover any work surface with newspapers or drop cloths.
• Always be sure to carefully read the label directions before opening the container. Procedures (and hazards) vary somewhat from product to product. In any case, open the container carefully, and bear in mind that you're dealing with a combination of powerful ingredients.
• Use your brush to spread a generous amount of remover onto the furniture. Use plenty, but don't overbrush. Or, you can pour the remover directly onto the horizontal surface of the piece, then spread the solution evenly with a brush.

Allow up to 30 minutes for the remover to work. Test its progress by scraping across the surface with a putty knife. If you strike bare wood, start scraping. Use a wide-blade scraper or putty knife to lift off the sludge. Keep the blade at a low angle to avoid scratching the wood. Clean off the residue with a pad of steel wool, lifting the pad often as you work and dipping it in water to remove the sludge. If you're using a water-soluble stripper, wash the piece with water. Do not use water on glue joints or veneered surfaces.

To clean round turnings, make a rope out of burlap or steel wool. Dip the rope in remover and pull it back and forth as you would a shoeshine rag. For carvings, use a wire or fiber brush with medium-size bristles. Toothbrushes and toothpicks are handy tools for hard-to-reach areas.

SANDING

The sanding stage of a refinishing project is crucial. The amount of sanding required depends on the condition of the piece. If the surface is badly dented or gouged, start with a coarse- to medium-grit abrasive. If you are using a belt sander, be careful not to apply too much pressure; the sander cuts quickly and can groove the surface of the wood. Unless you're a skilled sander, don't use a belt sander on veneer; you're likely to go right through the wood.

After sanding, remove dust and other residue as completely as possible. Wipe the surface with a cheesecloth rag dampened with mineral spirits, allow the surface to dry, then sand again with a medium- to fine-grit abrasive. The surface should now be smooth. Unless you plan to bleach or water-stain the wood, dampen the surface to raise the grain. Then use a very fine abrasive, and finish sanding the piece by hand.

STAINING AND BLEACHING

If you're not happy with the wood's natural hue, you can change the color with stain, or lighten it with bleach. Before applying the stain, first experiment with a small area that won't show. Remember that the color produced by a stain is determined by how long you let the stain penetrate the wood. The longer you leave the stain on before wiping, the darker the color will be.

Applying a commercial wood bleach is usually a two-step process, and often the bleach must stand overnight. Follow directions carefully. You also can use laundry bleach or oxalic acid, but they must be neutralized after an application with one part white vinegar or ammonia mixed with ten parts of water.

WOOD FINISHES

• *Varnish and polyurethane:* Like clear paint, varnish forms a hard, smooth surface on wood. Polyurethane is a sort of super varnish because it's impervious to liquids. And, although it's as hard as nails, polyurethane tends to flex as the wood expands and contracts. Varnish also is impervious to liquids, but it doesn't create as hard a finish as polyurethane does. Both varnish and polyurethane are applied with a brush and are available in gloss, satin, and matte finishes.
• *Lacquer:* This is a quick-drying finish that doesn't build up the thick coat that varnish or polyurethane does. Although lacquer is not as durable as varnish, it's easy to apply. One or two coats will create a clear finish while protecting the piece from wear and soil. Lacquer is best applied with a spray gun, but by working carefully and quickly, you can get good results with a fine, natural-bristle brush.
• *Shellac:* Clear or pigmented shellac produces a soft finish that is easily damaged by water but is also easy to repair. Always apply shellac with a new brush. Usually five to eight coats of shellac are necessary. Finish the job with a hard paste wax.
• *Oil:* Simple to apply, oil is often used to give furniture a beautiful bare-wood look. Although not as wear-proof as varnish, polyurethane, or lacquer, oil soaks into the wood grain to make the surface more durable. An oil finish is a good choice for fine furniture or pieces that don't get hard wear. To apply the first coat, pour the oil onto the wood surface and spread it evenly with a brush. When the surface is dry, sand it

lightly to remove the raised grain. Apply each subsequent coat with the grain, rubbing hard with a rag. A really fine oil finish may require six or eight applications. Using a commercial resin-oil finish speeds up the process. Whichever method you select, finish the job with hard wax after you've applied the final coat of oil.

APPLICATION

If you opt to finish the project with varnish, shellac, or lacquer, follow the manufacturer's directions for thinning and stirring, where applicable.

Dip a good-quality natural-bristle brush into the liquid until about one-third of the bristles are covered. Tap the brush on the side of the can to remove excess liquid, then gently brush the finish onto the wood surface. Drybrush over each completed area with long, overlapping strokes. Always brush with the grain of the wood, using just the tip of the bristles.

If air bubbles appear on the wood surface as you're applying the liquid, you may be bearing down too hard on the bristles. Wiping the bristles against the rim of the can or shaking the can before opening it can also cause bubbles to form. To eliminate bubbles from the wood surface, apply more of the finish and continue to brush until you work them out.

After each coat of varnish or shellac has completely dried, smooth it with fine sandpaper or steel wool. This ensures proper bonding between coats. Lacquer is the only clear finish that doesn't require sanding with steel wool between coats.

REPAIRS OF OLD PIECES

There are numerous rescue tactics for furniture in need of repair. Knowing a few simple fix-up techniques can transform a garage sale bargain into something special, or save a damaged piece of furniture from exile to the attic.

Here are some of the more common repair problems and tips on how to correct them:
• *Wobbly chairs:* A chair with the wobbles is begging to be repaired. To avoid mishap, remove the chair from circulation until it can be repaired.

Wobbling may be caused by one or more factors: The legs or stretchers may need regluing, or the holes into which the legs and stretchers fit may have become slightly enlarged. The "cure" in either case is fairly simple. First, use a towel-padded hammer to disassemble the chair. Be sure to label each piece with the name of the part for easy reassembly.

Next, remove all glue from both portions of each joint. Scrape off what you can, then sand off the rest. If, after sanding, the leg or stretcher fits too loosely in the holes, coat the joint with glue, then wrap with a layer of strong thread. Metal fasteners also are available for this purpose. To use fasteners, file down one side of the joint and tape the fastener in place.

Apply glue and tap the leg or stretcher into the receiving hole. Be careful no glue is left on the surface of the furniture. It will not accept stain and can ruin the final finish.

Draw joints tight by wrapping a rope or strong cord twice around the chair. Then, insert a small piece of wood between the two cords and turn it, tourniquet fashion, to tighten the ties.
• *Loose veneer:* If just a small area of veneer is loose, follow this simple procedure: Lift the loose edge and squirt in a dollop of white glue. Use a thin blade to spread the glue around. Place a piece of waxed paper over the glued area, then top with a board. Clamp the board securely with a C-clamp or weight it down with a pile of books.

If a large area of veneer is loose, or if you're replacing an entire section of veneer, use contact cement rather than white glue. Here's how to proceed:

Using a small brush, apply the cement to the veneer and

the undersurface. Allow the cement to dry for at least 30 minutes. Carefully lay the veneer in place. Strive for accuracy; you won't get a second chance. Then roll the veneered area with a rubber roller or a rolling pin.
• *Removing dents:* Select one of several techniques for dent removal, depending on the severity of the damage. For a slight dent, first try using stick shellac to fill in the dent. If that doesn't work, try this:

Use a needle to pierce tiny holes in the dented area. Dampen the dent with a few drops of water. After the wood swells, rub it lightly with rottenstone and oil.

If the furniture isn't severely dented and wood fibers aren't broken, try this repair technique:

Lay several folds of damp cloth over the damaged surface. Apply a hot iron to the cloth for several minutes. In many cases, the steam swells the wood fibers and returns them to their original state.

Steam will raise the grain of the wood surrounding the dent, so you will have to do a little extra sanding to smooth the surface before finishing.
• *Filling cracks:* A good wood putty, carefully applied, is great for filling in cracks. With a putty knife or small, thin-bladed knife, fill cracks with putty. Remove excess putty with a rag or fine sandpaper.
• *Repairing deep scratches:* To bandage a deep scratch on a piece of furniture you do not plan to refinish, try this: Touch up the area with a matching stain. With a tiny brush, fill the cavity with layers of shellac. Smooth the surface with extra-fine sandpaper and rub with rottenstone and oil.
• *Uncrazing a surface:* Too much exposure to the sun can cause a network of tiny cracks (crazing) in wood finishes. If the problem is not severe, use this method for eliminating crazing:

Rub the crazed area with steel wool, then polish with paste wax. If the crazing is severe, refinishing is the only way to restore surface beauty.

SLIPCOVER OR REUPHOLSTER?

Slipcovering does nothing more than cover existing upholstery. If the springs are in bad shape or the padding is exposed, a slipcover may not be the answer. However, if the piece is structurally sound, a slipcover is worth considering.

Ready-made slipcovers are the least expensive cover-ups, but the selection of fabrics, colors, and styles is limited. Most are made of knit fabric. If possible, opt for custom-made slipcovers. Though they cost more than ready-mades, they offer an infinitely wider range of fabric selection, and are much better looking in terms of styling and fit.

The price of your slipcover will depend largely on the quality and quantity of the fabric you choose. A standard sofa usually requires 15 to 20 yards of fabric.

The major advantage of slipcovers is that they can be removed and cleaned or washed. Slipcovering is also great for just a quick-and-easy face-lift for an upholstered piece. One disadvantage is that covers are usually made of lightweight fabric, so they are apt to show wear more quickly than upholstery fabric.

Reupholstery gives you a new look for your furniture— permanently, or at least until the fabric wears out. One of the nicest things about reupholstering is that, as a rule, any necessary repair work on the padding and springs is figured into the cost. New cushions are extra.

Prices for reupholstering vary greatly, with fabric and labor charges being the main variables. Most reupholstery fabrics have to be ordered, and there often is a long wait for delivery. Sometimes it's possible to save time and money by buying your fabric from the shop where the upholstery work is being done.

Whatever you decide, it's a good idea to shop around. Get recommendations from friends, check fabric quality, and, if possible, see examples of finished work.

CARE AND CLEANING

Proper care and cleaning are essential to the longevity and lasting good looks of all kinds of furniture—wood, upholstered, plastic, wicker, metal, and others. Here are some preventive maintenance tips you'll want to keep in mind.

WOOD FURNITURE

Wood is extremely sensitive to excessive heat, humidity, and dryness. If your house is prone to any of these climatic problems, you'd be wise to have them corrected. Failure to do so is apt to cause serious structural damage to wood pieces, and repairs can be quite costly. Warping and splitting of wood pieces are the two most common problems caused by too much or too little moisture in the air.

Dusting is another element of preventive maintenance for wood. Dust frequently, but be sure you're not harming the surface while removing abrasive particles. Always dust with the grain of the wood and lift objects so you can dust underneath. Never slide them around or you may scratch the surface.

Avoid using cheesecloth as a dustcloth unless you're sure the sizing has been washed out. And don't expect a feather duster to really dust. It will push dust around, but not pick it up. A polish-treated cloth is good for a polished finish, but it may soften wax on a waxed finish.

Polish and wax only once every few months and use only polishes recommended for furniture. Always follow directions on labels and pre-test any new wax or polish on a small out-of-the-way area.

Various wood finishes require different treatments. Here's a guide to follow:
• *High-gloss finishes* may be maintained with either a liquid polish or a paste wax. Let liquid dry, then buff. Paste wax requires rubbing to bring out the sheen.
• *Satin-gloss finishes.* Use a cleaning polish or cream wax without silicone.
• *Low-gloss finish.* Use a liquid polish designed for low-luster wood or a cleaning wax that removes surface soil and protects the finish without producing a shine.
• *Oil finishes.* Wash periodically with a mild soap solution to which a few drops of mineral spirits or lemon juice have been added. Then apply boiled linseed oil. Dust the piece with a cloth dampened with clean water and glycerine or mineral thinner.
• *Painted finishes.* Wipe with a cloth or sponge dampened in a mild soap and water solution. Avoid wax or liquid polish unless the label states that it is recommended for painted surfaces.
• *Antique furniture* should be cared for the same way as high-gloss finishes. Avoid a heavy buildup of wax.

UPHOLSTERED FURNITURE

The best way to maintain upholstered pieces is to vacuum once a week and turn the cushions to distribute wear.

When a general cleaning is needed, check the fiber content of the fabric to see how it will react to shampooing. Always pretest each color in your upholstery to make sure there is no bleeding. (Test inconspicuous areas of the upholstered piece.)

After making sure that your furniture can be safely shampooed, clean it with one of the spray foam cleaners on the market, or create your own home formula. Never use soap on upholstered furniture; it doesn't rinse off well and the soapy residue tends to attract soil.

Make a dry foam using a synthetic detergent and warm (never hot) water. Whip the solution until you can apply only the foam to a small area at a time. Use a soft-bristled brush or a sponge. Work quickly, scrubbing with a circular motion. Lift off dirty suds with a rubber spatula, dry sponge, or clean towel. Rinse with a clean cloth dipped in warm water and wrung almost dry.

Dry the furniture as quickly as possible by opening the windows or using a fan.

Fabrics that aren't to be shampooed should be dry cleaned with a no-water cleaning solution. Be sure to read the instructions carefully and apply sparingly.

If you're at all unsure about do-it-yourself upholstery cleaning, then by all means, have the job done professionally.

PLASTIC FURNITURE

You can keep plastic pieces clean and looking their best by wiping them with a cloth dampened in water or a gentle liquid detergent solution. Never use abrasive cleaners or furniture polish on plastic. Some manufacturers recommend automobile wax as a deterrent against the minor scratches that plastic furniture can acquire.

WICKER FURNITURE

Protect your wicker furniture by using it only indoors, or on a sheltered porch or covered patio. Rain and direct sunlight can damage wicker.

Use a vacuum cleaner brush attachment to remove dust from woven areas. To clean, wipe the furniture with a water-dampened cloth or wash with a soapy sponge. Rinse the furniture thoroughly, then wipe it dry. Rub on liquid furniture wax for sheen and extra surface protection.

RATTAN FURNITURE

This type of furniture is made from a natural material that, like wood, needs moisture. If seating pieces snap and crackle with pressure, the furniture is calling for help.

To clean, wipe with a slightly dampened sponge, being careful not to wet the frame or penetrate the weave. Or spray a fine mist with a plant sprayer, then wipe it off with a cloth. Let rattan furniture dry before using.

OUTDOOR METAL FURNITURE

Protect aluminum by spraying it with a clear lacquer two or three times every summer. Dull, unpainted aluminum can be restored by rubbing it with fine steel wool dipped in kerosene. Color-coated aluminum (and webbing) can be washed with a mild detergent solution. Rinse it well, then apply automobile paste wax to the aluminum.

Wrought-iron furniture retains its good looks if kept painted with good exterior oil enamel in a gloss finish. This prevents rust and makes the furniture easy to clean.

REDWOOD FURNITURE

To prevent darkening of the soft redwood color, apply one or two coats of preservative to keep out the moisture.

Before application, scrub the surface with detergent, rinse well, and let dry.

If redwood has been stained, then waxed, all you need to do is wipe it with a damp sponge.

FURNITURE FIRST AID

TYPE OF FINISH	PROCEDURE: SCRATCH REMOVAL
Plastic	Regular applications of automobile wax fill in minor scratches.
Dark Wood	Rub nutmeats (walnut, Brazil, or butternut) into scratch, or touch up with furniture crayon, eyebrow pencil, or shoe polish in a shade to match finish.
Mahogany or Cherry	Apply aged or darkened iodine.
Maple	Apply aged or darkened iodine diluted 50 percent with denatured alcohol.
Oil	Using a fine steel-wool pad, rub lightweight mineral oil, boiled linseed oil, or paraffin oil into scratch. Wipe dry.

TYPE OF STAIN	PROCEDURE: STAIN REMOVAL
Water Marks or Rings	Place clean, thick blotter over stain and press down with a warm iron. Repeat. If that fails, try application of cleaning polish or wax. Or apply camphorated oil with a lint-free cloth, rubbing with the wood grain. Wipe dry. Repeat.
White Marks	Rub with thin paste of wax and mineral spirits. When dry, apply thin coat of wax or cleaning polish. Or rub with cigar or cigarette ashes, using cloth dipped in wax, vegetable shortening, lard, salad oil, or lubricating oil. Wipe off immediately. Rewax.
Milk or Alcohol	Using fingers, rub liquid or paste wax into area. If that fails, rub in paste of boiled linseed oil and rottenstone (available at most hardware stores). Use powdered pumice for dull finishes. Wipe dry. Polish. Or apply ammonia with damp cloth. Polish immediately.
Cigarette Burns	Rub area with scratch-concealing polish. If that fails, apply rottenstone paste as for alcohol stain. If burn is deep, area may have to be refinished.
Heat Marks	Rub area gently with dry steel-wool soap pad a tiny area at a time, wiping up powdery substance. If this fails, rub with cloth dampened in camphorated oil or mineral spirits. Rub dry with clean cloth. Repeat. Or rub gently with fine steel wool. Wipe off. Repolish.
Sticking Paper	Saturate paper with lightweight oil. Wait. Rub area gently with fine steel wool. Wipe dry.
Nail Polish	Rub area gently with fine steel wood dipped in liquid wax. Wipe away polish. Rewax.
Paint Spots	If paint is wet, treat like nail polish stain. If dry, soak area with linseed oil. Wait until paint softens. Wipe away paint with cloth dampened in linseed oil. If any paint remains, apply paste of boiled linseed oil and rottenstone.
Candle Wax	Harden wax with ice cube, catching moisture as ice melts. Using fingers, crumble off wax. Scrape remaining wax gently with old credit card. Rub with cloth dampened in mineral spirits. Or place clean, thick blotter over stain and press down with warm iron. Rub area with liquid polish. Wipe dry.

SHELVING SUGGESTIONS

Shelves are the answer when storage space is in short supply. Every room in the house can benefit from their presence, and they needn't be elaborate or expensive to be effective. The information provided here is intended to help you design and install shelves that will best suit your particular storage needs.

Advance planning is a good idea if you want your shelf project to function well. First decide what it is you're going to put on the shelves. Size and weight of objects will (or should) influence the kind of building materials and hardware you choose.

SHELF HARDWARE

The success of any shelving project rests, quite literally, upon its support system. As a rule, the heaviest articles stored on shelves are books, records, and stereo gear. Books of average size covering a square foot of shelf space weigh approximately 20 pounds; a linear foot of 12-inch record albums weighs 45 pounds. So ask yourself these questions before making your choice. What weights and spans must the hardware hold? Can shelves be supported at the ends, or must they be rear-mounted? Do you want fixed or adjustable brackets? How will you attach the shelves to the wall?

Once you've answered the questions about the mechanics, consider appearance. Styling ranges from strictly utilitarian to handsome hardwood wall systems. You'll discover that price is a relevant factor, too—the hardware sometimes costs more than the lumber for the shelves.

The illustrations *at right* show the eight most commonly used support systems, but there are many variations. With standards and brackets, for instance, you can choose painted or plated finishes, different bracket shapes and locking mechanisms, and such specialties as angled supports for magazine racks.

While you're selecting hardware, give some thought to buying prefinished shelving. Though considerably more expensive than ordinary lumber or plywood, it saves a lot of tedious work.

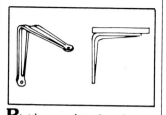

Rigid pressed-steel angle brackets hold medium-weight loads. Always mount them with the longer leg against the wall. For heavier duty, choose brackets that are reinforced with triangular gussets between the legs (not shown).

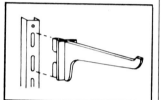

Brackets clip into slotted standards, allowing you to adjust the spacing between shelves. Choose 8-, 10-, or 12-inch brackets. Properly installed, this system supports surprisingly heavy loads to satisfy a variety of needs.

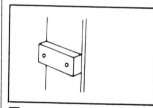

The simplest (and least expensive) way to hold shelves inside closets, bookcases, or cabinets is to install cleats at each end. For longer spans, attach a third strip to the unit's back to support the rear of the shelves.

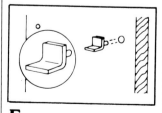

For a dressier look, mount shelves by popping pin-type clips into predrilled holes. Relatively inexpensive, they'll support heavy loads on ¾-inch-thick boards up to about 30 inches long.

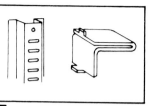

To make end-mounted shelves adjustable, use standards and clips such as these. Here again, limit the spans to about 30 inches. For a flush installation, you can dado the standards into the sides of the cabinet.

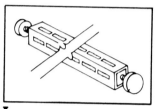

In situations where you can't or don't want to make holes in the walls, use "tension" poles. They work by expansion, wedging between the floor and ceiling, and are relatively inexpensive.

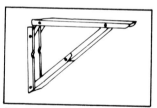

Folding brackets let you drop a shelf out of the way when it's not in use. You can buy a variation of folding brackets for spring-loaded typewriter-style installations (not shown); the shelf pops up when you pull it from a cabinet.

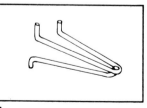

Light-duty wire brackets are among the many accessories you can mount on perforated hardboard. Measure the board's thickness before you buy; ¼- and ⅛-inch sizes require different devices.

PUTTING UP SHELF STRIPS

Bracket shelving seems to concentrate a lot of weight on the few small fasteners that secure the strips. But those fasteners don't actually bear the load—they simply clamp the strips to the wall. This means that the strength of a shelving system depends more on the fasteners' holding power than it does on their size.

Use plastic anchors only for light-duty installations. Wood screws driven directly into studs hold much better —but if you use them, you must adjust your design according to the way the wall was framed. Hollow-wall fasteners such as toggle and expansion bolts let you put strips precisely where you want them.

Armed with the proper fasteners and a screwdriver, drill, and level, you can hang the strips in an hour or so. Generally, it's best to plumb the strips so they'll be perfectly vertical. However, if you have walls that are out of square, you may have to measure from floor or ceiling

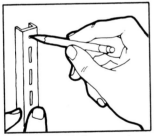

to make the shelving aesthetically acceptable.

Before hanging the first strip, note whether it has a definite top and bottom (sketch 1). Mark and drill for

the top hole only. Insert a bolt (sketch 2), but don't tighten it until you've plumbed the strip, drilled the remaining holes, and installed the lower bolt or bolts. Draw a level line from the strip's

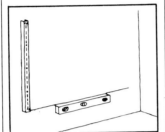

top or bottom to locate the last strip (sketch 3). Again, remember that if your walls are out of square, you may have to measure from floor to ceiling. Lastly, position the intermediate strips, using the

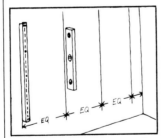

line you've drawn as a guide (sketch 4). Be sure to maintain equal spacing between the strips.

Plot your shelf layout carefully, using graph paper and the dimensions *at right* to minimize "surprises" later.

The span table gives the maximum distance you should allow between supports. It allows for a full load of books or records, which are the heaviest items you're likely to put on shelves. Don't let the unsupported ends of the shelves extend more than half the span distance beyond the last support, or they may begin to bow.

With adjustable shelving, you can save space and reduce dusting time by tailoring vertical spacings to exactly accommodate your possessions.

Just be sure to leave an extra inch or two so you can easily tip out a book or record (allow a little more leeway if you decide on fixed shelves).

Before determining your final layout, consult the lower table *below* for the spacing required between shelves for several often-shelved items.

SHELVING SPANS

Material Used	Maximum Span
¾-inch plywood	36″
¾-inch particleboard	28″
1x12 lumber	24″
2x10 or 2x12 lumber	48-56″
½-inch acrylic	22″
½-inch glass	18″

(Assumes shelves fully loaded with books)

SHELF SPACING GUIDE

Item	Space Required
Paperback books	8″
Hardback books	11″
Oversize books	15″
Catalog-format books	15½″
Record albums	13½″
8-track tapes	6¼″
Cassette tapes	5″
Circular slide trays	9¾″

Miscellaneous
LAMPS/WIRING TIPS

A little knowledge of electrical wiring techniques can save you a lot of money. Though complicated projects are best left to professional electricians, there's no reason to shy away from creating your own floor and table lamps, rewiring old or broken lamps, or replacing old ceiling fixtures. This simple step-by-step wiring guide will help get you started.

HOW TO WIRE A LAMP

Just about anything hollow or with a hole through its center can be converted into a lamp. Basic lamp wiring is quickly learned, and the required components are readily available at lamp and fixture stores. As shown in the drawing, *below,* most table lamps are comprised of a *body,* a *base,* and a *harp* that supports the shade. Working parts include a *plug, cord,* and *socket.* The cord runs through a *threaded rod* concealed within the lamp body.

With a swag lamp, *below,* the cord is threaded through a chain that is attached to a *loop.* This loop is connected to a socket with a *nipple.* Toggle or *screw hangers* and *hooks* hold the chain; a *switch* controls the light.

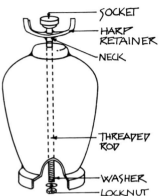

1. To wire the lamp, first feed the rod up through the base and into the body. Secure the rod at the bottom with a *locknut* and *washer* or with two *lamp nuts*; at the top, secure with a decorative *knurled nut* or *threaded neck.* Fit a *harp retainer* over the threaded rod, then screw on a *socket base* and your main assembly job is complete.

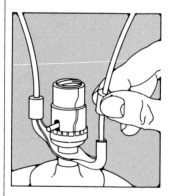

UNDERWRITERS KNOT

2. If the lamp you're working with has a short body, you'll probably be able to simply push the cord up through the rod. But if the body is tall, you may have to run stiff wire through first, then pull the cord through. Next, tie an *Underwriters knot* at the top as shown. It's a good idea to secure the cord below with a second knot.

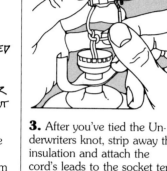

3. After you've tied the Underwriters knot, strip away the insulation and attach the cord's leads to the socket terminals. Attach the plug to the opposite end. *Round-cord* and *flat-cord* plugs are suitable for most lamps, but some newer lamps require *polarized* plugs. If you're not certain which type is best, ask your lamp store dealer.

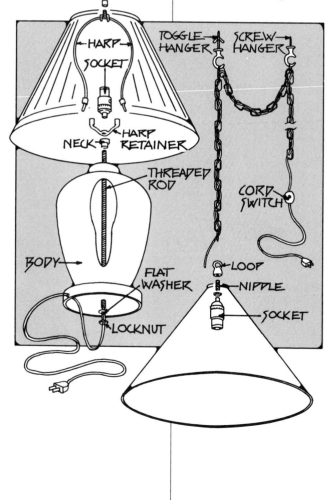

4. Finally, reassemble the socket and install the harp as shown. The two most commonly used harps are the two-piece detachable harp and the one-piece screw-on harp, which screws directly onto the top housing of a socket. Add a bulb and a shade, and your lamp is ready for use.

REPLACING A FIXTURE

Substituting a new fixture for an old one usually takes just a few minutes if you have the proper hardware.

First, be sure to eliminate any possibility of electrical shock. Shut off the power at the service panel, then double-check with your tester before touching the fixture. Wall switches interrupt only the fixture's "hot" wire, so you still could get a shock through the neutral wire if the circuit is live.

Next, determine how the old fixture is attached. Support systems vary but all systems secure the fixture to its electrical box—usually a four-inch octagon—and in some cases to the ceiling as well. Some fixtures secure with bolts to a *strap*; others mount with a *hickey* to a *stud* in the center of the box; and still others use a combination of these support systems.

After you've dealt with the preliminaries mentioned above, simply follow the steps illustrated here. Take care not to undo any other connections you may find in the electrical box.

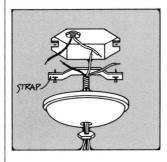

1. As you dismantle the old fixture, note how the components fit together; take particular notice of how the *leads* are affixed. The leads serve as the cord, connecting the socket to the house wiring.

2. Strip about ¾ inch from the new fixture's leads. You can distinguish lead wires by their black and white colors. If the wires are stranded, twist the ends slightly.

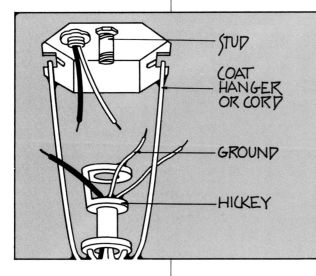

3. Provide temporary support for heavy fixtures with a coat hanger or strong cord. Keep temporary suspension time to a minimum by pre-assembling all of the components before attempting to hang the fixture.

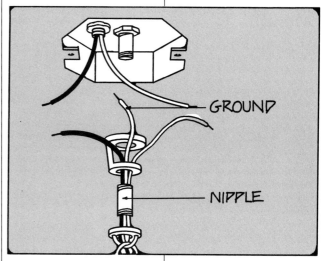

4. Make certain all of the wires exit through the side of the hickey. Then screw a nipple into the hickey and thread the hickey onto the stud. Alternative mounting systems

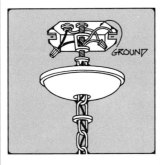

5. After the fixture is mechanically secure, make the electrical connections. Without exception, same color wires go together: white to white, black to black. Use solderless connectors or cone-shaped wire nuts to make the connections. Next, carefully coil up the wires within the housing box.

include a *strap*, or metal plate (drawing 1), which is required if the holes in the fixture's canopy don't match those in the box.

6. Install bulbs, then screw or bolt the lamp fixture to the ceiling or wall. Turn the main circuit back on. If the light doesn't work, first make certain the bulbs are good, then turn off the main circuit and disassemble the fixture. Check all of the connections to see if the wires are crossed, if the wires are in contact, and if all points of connection are properly insulated.

PICTURE-HANGING TIPS

For most people, it's no easy matter determining the best way to hang framed art work and other items—big and small. If the old hammer and nail routine has you stymied, perhaps one of these hang-up ideas will offer the solution you're looking for.

LIGHT WEIGHTS

Hanging lightweight objects is easy on a hollow wall. Anything weighing up to 10 pounds can be hung from nails, even on drywall. For framed items, two nails or hooks are better than one, because they give more support and keep the frame from shifting on the wall.

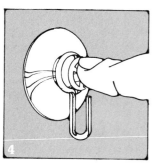

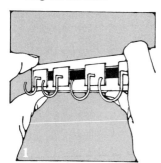

Adhesive fixtures come in various shapes and sizes, and are ideal for lightweight use.
• *Self-adhesive hanging tracks* (1) have a peel-and-stick backing, and are great for holding lightweight items such as ties, jewelry, and keys.
• *Gummed picture hangers* (2) can be used for items weighing less than three pounds.
• *Self-adhesive hooks* (3) are popular for use in closets, bathrooms, and mudrooms.

One word of caution about adhesives: They need several hours to set between installation and use. When it's time for removal, pry the fixture away from the wall with a sharp knife.

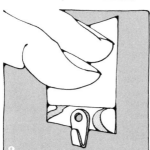

• *Suction cup fixtures* (4) cause the least amount of damage to walls, and provide a fast way to hang items on a smooth, nonporous surface. But beware: Even when moistened for a better grip, these fixtures eventually lose their suction power and fall from the wall.

MEDIUM WEIGHTS

If you need to hang heavier items, such as mirrors (up to 25 pounds), there are various ways to do so.
• *Dry-wall hangers* (5) are especially designed for plasterboard walls. No tools are required for an easy-and-fast installation; the pointed end of the hanger simply twists into the hollow wall.

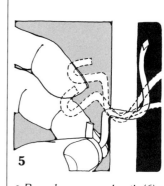

• *Brass hangers and nails* (6) come prepackaged according to weight, and require only a few taps of the hammer to install. Large-size hangers and nails can hold items weighing up to 100 pounds.

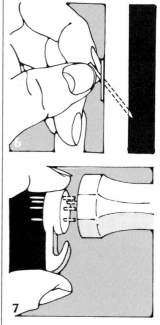

• *Hard surface hangers and loops* (7) can be hammered into concrete, cinder block, hardwood, and soft brick. If you need to hang something on a hard brick wall, try a masonry nail.

HEAVY WEIGHTS

To hang heavy objects on hollow walls, doors, and ceilings, you'll need a drill, a screwdriver, and anchors.

• *Metal expansion anchors* (8) have a shaft that spreads out like an umbrella and grips the back side of the wall when the bolt in the center is screwed in tightly. Some types can be hammered into the wall.

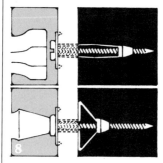

• *Toggle bolts* (9) support heavy loads but require bigger holes than expansion hangers. To install, drill hole; fold hinged wings together; push bolt and wings through

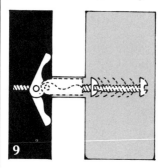

the hole until the wings open. One problem: The object has to be held in place at the same time the toggle bolt is installed.
• *Combination bolts* (10) are a cross between expansion anchors and toggle bolts, and are designed to be used in hollow, thick, or solid walls, or wherever you wish to avoid making a large hole.

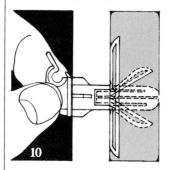

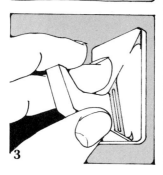

Credits

DESIGNERS AND ARCHITECTS

The following is a list by page number of the interior designers, architects, and project designers whose work appears in this book.

Pages 10-11
Robert E. Dittmer
Pages 20-21
Robert E. Dittmer
Pages 24-25
Robert Zoller and Kim R. Williamson, ASID
Page 26
Jerry Ross and Debbie Schmitz
Page 30-31
Marthe Jocelyn
Pages 32-33
Linda Carbutt/ Now & Then
Page 34
(Top): Carol Miller, ASID, The Bird House
(Bottom): Ted Kloss
Page 35
Robert E. Dittmer
Pages 36-37
Architect: Ronald F. Katz
Page 38
Pamela Hughes
Page 39
(Top): Ann Vander-warker
(Bottom): Architects: Bruno Ast, Gunduz Dagdelen
Page 40
Tom Boccia
Page 41
Don Bailey and Keith Gasser. Location: Baltimore Symphony Decorator's Show-house
Pages 42-49
Robert E. Dittmer
Pages 50-51
Liz Jones, E.B. Williamson—Jones Interior Design; Atlanta Decorator Showhouse
Pages 52-53
Kris Derdivanis, Color Design Art

Pages 54-55
Robert E. Dittmer
Pages 56-57
Barbara Epstein
Pages 58-59
Robert E. Dittmer
Page 60
Katie Ragsdale
Page 62
Sara Jane Treinen
Page 63
(Top): Emerson Interiors
(Bottom): George Hans
Page 64
(Bottom): R. Halpren-Ruder/Barbara S. Malone
Page 65
Don's Color Center
Page 67
David and Beverly Grant
Pages 68-69
Patricia Gwilliam
Pages 72-73
Suzy Taylor, ASID
Pages 76-77
Rebecca Jerdee
Page 78
(chest) Leslie Stiles
(floor) Suzy Taylor, ASID
Pages 80-81
Robert E. Dittmer
Pages 82-83
Christine Garrett
Page 84
(Top): Savannah Lane, Inc.; Baltimore Symphony Decora-tor's Showhouse
(Bottom): Robert E. Dittmer
Page 85
Lorri Anderson, ASID, and Cheryl Hillbrook
Page 86
Robert E. Dittmer
Page 87
Paul Marchetti
Pages 88-93
Robert E. Dittmer
Page 96
John Baker
Page 98
Kate Wharton/ Now & Then
Page 99
Muriel Hebert
Page 100
(Top): Rebecca Jerdee
(Bottom): Robert E. Dittmer
Page 101
Bruce Bierman
Page 102
Sharon Schnackenberg

Page 103
Barbara J. Rocha, The House Dressers
Page 104
Karin Weller
Page 105
(Top right): Judith Flamenbaum
(Bottom left): Muriel Hebert
Page 121
Ron Sorenson
Page 123
(Bottom): David Ashe
Page 124
Jane Wienner
Page 125
(Top): Ciba Vaughan
(Bottom): Robert Pfreundschuh
Page 126
(Bottom): The Design Concern
Page 127
Suzy Taylor, ASID
Page 128
Quilt: courtesy of Made in America
Page 129
Sunny and Clay Henderson
Page 130
Lilian Silberman
Page 131
(Top): Gary Boling
Page 132
Marthe Jocelyn
Page 133
Ciba Vaughan
Page 135
(Top): Robert Chodzinski
Page 136
(Top): Pamela Bookey
(Bottom): Ben Ardery
Page 137
(Top): John McNamara
(Bottom): Jean Chappell Interiors
Page 138
(Top right): Lawrence E. King, Jim Mince-moyer, Lee Schmidt
Page 139
Sunny and Clay Henderson
Page 141
James Miles
Page 142
Dave Ashe
Page 144
(Bottom): Stephen P. Mead

Page 145
Richard Bettini
Page 148
(Top): Dustin Davis
(Bottom): Ciba Vaughan
Page 149
(Bottom): David Ashe
Page 150
Kevin Walz
Page 152
Teri Peters
Page 158-159
Molly Epstein

PHOTOGRAPHERS

We extend our thanks to the following photographers whose work appears in this book.

Ernest Braun
George de Gennaro
Mike Dieter
Peter M. Fine
Harry Hartman
Jim Hedrich, Hedrich-Blessing
Bill Helms
Thomas E. Hooper
William N. Hopkins
David Jordan
Armen Kachaturian
Fred Lyon
Maris/Semel
E. Alan McGee
Tom Miyassaki
Bradley Olman
Lilo Raymond
Jessie Walker

FIELD EDITORS

Our thanks to the Better Homes and Gardens Field Editors for their valuable as-sistance in locating homes for photography.

Pat Carpenter
Barbara Cathcart
Eileen Alexandra Deymier
Estelle Bond Guralnick
Sharon Haven
Helen Heitkamp
Bonnie Maharam
Ruth L. Reiter
Maxine Schweiker
Mary Anne Thomson
Jessie Walker
Bonnie Warren

Index

Page numbers in *italics* refer to illustrations or to illustrated text.